RACE RELATIONS IN EMPLOYMENT LAW

Copyright © Ryan Clement 2023

All Rights Reserved

No part of this publication may be reproduced or transmitted
in any form or by any means, electronic, mechanical,
photocopying, recording or otherwise, or stored
in any retrieval system of any nature
without permission
in writing from both the copyright owner
or
a licence permitting restricted copying in the United Kingdom
issued by the Copyright Licensing Agency

First Edition (2021)
Second Edition (2023)

RACE RELATIONS IN EMPLOYMENT LAW

*This book is dedicated to my late mother,
Ann, and my son, Kofi.*

Acknowledgements

I give a special thanks to Andey for reading and commenting on the draft, suggesting amendments and edits, and to ART for designing the book covers. Also, a special thanks to Caz for her work on Chapter One.

About the Author

Ryan Clement, LL.M., BA, BSc, FRSA, was born in Chiswick, London. He is a barrister and has written many published articles.

www.ryanclement.com

CONTENTS

Preface to First Edition

Preface to Second Edition

Introduction

Chapter One

How it all began, **1.1-1.20**

Chapter Two

Equality Act 2010, **2.1**

- *Race*, **2.2-12**

- *Direct Discrimination*, **2.13-21**

- *Indirect Discrimination*, **2.22-27**

- *Indirect Discrimination compared with Discrimination*, **2.28-31**

- *Harassment*, **2.32-42**

- *Harassment and Direct Discrimination*, **2.43**

- *Victimisation*, **2.44-48**

- *Direct Discrimination and Victimisation*, **2.49**

- *Racism and Race Discrimination*, **2.51**

- *Institutional Racism*, **2.52-53**

Chapter Three

Grievance & Disciplinary, **3.1**

- *Grievance*, **3.1-13**

- *ACAS Code*, **3.5-6**

- *Written Statement of Particulars of Employment*, **3.14-15**

- *The Grievance*, **3.16-19**

- *Formal Grievance Process and Procedure*, **3.20-22**

- *Grievance Letter*, **3.23-24**

- *Invitation to Disciplinary Letter*, **3.26**

- *Disciplinary Procedure and Process*, **3.27-3.33**

- *Investigation (disciplinary)*, **3.30**

- *Disciplinary Procedure*, **3.31-33**

- *Conduct done in the course of employment*, **3.34**

Chapter Four

Employment Tribunal I, **4.1-37**

- *Notifying ACAS*, **4.3**

- *Time limits*, **4.4**

- *Three months less 1 day*, **4.5-8**

- *Claim Form (ET1)*, **4.9-11**

- *Response (ET3)*, **4.12-14**

- *Pleadings*, **4.15-17**

- *Direct discrimination (Claimant)*, **4.18**

- *Direct discrimination (Respondent)*, **4.19**

- *Indirect discrimination (Claimant)*, **4.20-21**

- *Indirect discrimination (Respondent)*, **4.22-23**

- *Harassment (Claimant)*, **4.24-26**

- *Harassment (Respondent)*, **4.27-28**

- *Victimisation (Claimant)*, **4.29-30**

- *Victimisation (Respondent)*, **4.31-33**

- *Employer's liability*, **4.34**

- *Statutory Defence*, **4.35-36**

- *Territorial Jurisdiction*, **4.37**

- *Jurisdiction – discrimination by non-employers,* **4.38-41**

Chapter Five

Pleadings, **5.1-13**

- *Grounds of Complaint (Claims 1-4)*, **5.2-3, 5.5-6, 5.8-9, 5.11-12**

- *Grounds of Resistance (Claims 1-4)*, **5.2, 5.4-5, 5.7-8, 5.10-11, 5.13**

- *Amending the Claim*, **5.14-23**

Chapter Six

Employment Tribunal II, **6.1-47**

- *List of issues (Claims 1-4)*, **6.5**

- *Strike out/deposit orders*, **6.9**

- *Tribunal Orders*, **6.10**

- *Disclosure*, **6.11-12**

- *Bundle,* **6.13**

- *Witness statements,* **6.14-16**

- *Mediation,* **6.17-20**

- *(Mediation) In the workplace,* **6.18**

- *Employment Tribunal Service – Judicial Mediation,* **6.19-20**

- *Settlement Agreement/Without prejudice offer/COT3,* **6.21-25**

- *Without prejudice save as to costs,* **6.26**

- *The Hearing,* **6.27-37**

- *Remedy,* **6.38-44**

- *Reconsideration and Appeal (EAT),* **6.45-47**

Chapter Seven

Diversity Awareness & Inclusion, **7.1-14**

- *Social Construct,* **7.5-7**

- *Inclusion,* **7.8-14**

Chapter Eight

Institutional racism, **8.1-38**

- *Crown Prosecution Service in 2001,* **8.5-6**

- *Independent review into racism in Scottish cricket – 2022,* **8.8-11**

- *London Fire Brigade (Independent Culture Review),* **8.12**

- *Yorkshire County Cricket Club,* **8.13-22**

- *Conclusion,* **8.23-38**

Chapter Nine

Training, **9.1-15**

- Questions, **9.16**

Chapter Ten

Statutes, Rules, Regulations & Links, **10.1-4**

- Equality Act 2010 (Key Extracts), **10.1**

- Employment Tribunals Act 1996 – ACAS Certificate before instituting proceedings, **10.2**

- Employment Appeal Tribunal Rules 1993, **10.3**

- The Employment Tribunals Rules of Procedure 2013, Schedule 1, **10.4**

- Websites, **10.5**

CASES

(1) Armitage, (2) Marsden and (3) H M Prison Service (appellants) v. Johnson (respondent) [1997] IRLR 162, **6.39**

Arvunescu (appellant) v Quick Release (Automotive) Ltd (respondent) [2023] IRLR 230; [2023] ICR 271; [2022] EWCA Civ 1600, **6.22.1-4**

Ayodele (appellant) v Citylink Ltd and another (respondents) [2018] IRLR 114; [2018] ICR 748; [2017] EWCA Civ 1913, **6.14.1**

Base Childrenswear Ltd (appellant) v Otshudi (respondent) [2020] IRLR 118; [2019] EWCA Civ 1648, **6.14.1**

Bathgate (appellant) v Technip UK Ltd and others (respondents) [2022] EAT 155; [2023] IRLR 4, **6.22.4, 6.25.1-3**

Beneviste v Kingston University [2006] UKEAT/0393/05, **2.47**

Blackburn v Aldi Stores [2013] IRLR 846, **3.8**

British Airways plc (appellants) v Starmer (respondent) [2005] IRLR 862, **2.4**

Chandhok and another v Tirkey (Equality and Human Rights Commission intervening) [2015; IRLR 195; [2015] ICR 527; (2014) UKEAT/0190/14, **2.12.1**

Commission for Racial Equality (appellants/plaintiffs) v. Dutton (respondent/defendant) [1989] IRLR 8, **2.9**

Commissioners of Inland Revenue and another (appellants) v Morgan (respondent) [2002] IRLR 776, **8.1, 8.24, 8.27.3**

Commissioner of Police of the Metropolis v Shaw [2012] ICR 464, **6.40**

Dawkins (appellant) v Department of the Environment sub nom Crown Suppliers PSA (respondents) [1993] IRLR 284, **2.9**

De Souza v Vinci Construction (UK) Ltd [2017] EWCA Civ 879, **6.42**

Durrani v London Borough of Ealing UKEAT/0454/2012/RN, (Transcript), **4.29**

Essop and others v Home Office (UK Border Agency) [2017] UKSC 27, **2.31**

Forbes (appellant) v LHR Airport Ltd (respondent) [2019] IRLR 890, **3.34, 4.36**

Grant v South-West Trains Ltd [1998] IRLR 188, **3.10**

Grant (appellant) v. HM Land Registry (respondent) and Equality and Human Rights Commission (interverner) [2011] IRLR 748, **2.81, 4.28**

Ishola v Transport for London [2020] EWCA Civ 112, **2.27**

Iwuchukwu v City Hospitals Sunderland NHS Foundation Trust [2019] IRLR 1022; [2019] EWCA Civ 498, **4.29**

Law v Wirral Golf Club (Preliminary Hearing), Case No. 2405273/2016, Liverpool ET, 20 April 2017, **4.2**

Lawson (appellant) v. Serco Ltd (respondents); Botham (appellant) v. Ministry of Defence (respondents); Crofts and others (respondents) v. Veta Ltd and others (appellants) [2006] IRLR 289, **4.37**

Mandla v Lee [1983] ICR 385, **2.5, 2.7**

Michalak (respondent) v General Medical Council and others (appellants) [2018] IRLR 60; [2018] ICR 49; [2017] UKSC 71; [2018] 1 All ER 463; [2017] 1 WLR 4193, **4.40**

Naeem v Secretary of State for Justice [2017] UKSC 27, **2.31**

Nazir and another v Asim - [2010] ICR 1225, **2.40**

Nagarajan (appellant) v. London Regional Transport (respondents) [1999] IRLR 572, **8.3, 8.5**

Northern Joint Police Board (appellants) v Power (respondent) [1997] IRLR 610, **2.4, 2.10**

Onu (appellant) v. Akwiwu and another (respondents); Taiwo (appellant) v. Olaigbe and another (respondents) [2016] IRLR 719; [2016] ICR 756; [2016] UKSC 31, **2.9.1**

Orphanos (Appellant) v. Queen Mary College (Respondents) [1985] IRLR 349, **2.5**

Owen & Briggs v James (CA) [1982] ICR 618, **8.1**

Richmond Pharmacology v Dhaliwal [2009] ICR 724, **4.26**

Royal Mail Group Ltd (Respondent) v Efobi (Appellant) [2021] UKSC 33, **6.14**

Seide (appellant) v Gillette Industries Ltd (respondents) [1980] IRLR 427, **2.9**

Selkent Bus Co. Ltd v Moore [1996] ICR 836, **5.18-19**

Taylor v Secretary of State for Scotland (HL) [2000] ICR 595, **3.10**

The Law Society and others (appellants) v. Bahl (respondent) [2003] IRLR 640, **2.15, 2.17**

Transport for London v Aderemi (2011) UKEAT/0006/11, **8.27.1-2**

Vento v Chief Constable of West Yorkshire Police (No.2) [2002] EWCA Civ 1871, [2003] IRLR 102, [2003] ICR 318, **6.42**

WA Goold (Pearmark) Ltd (appellants) v. McConnell and another (respondents) [1995] IRLR 516, **3.7, 3.12, 3.13**

Warby v Wunda Group plc UKEAT/0434/11/CEA (Transcript), **2.39**

West Midlands Passenger Transport Executive v Singh [1988] IRLR 186, **9.7**

LEGISLATION, RULES, CODES, REGULATIONS ETC.

Legislation
Disability Discrimination Act 1995, **Introduction**
Employment Rights Act 1996,
    s.1, **3.12, 3.14**
    s.3(1)(b)(ii), **3.15**
    s.3(1)(c), **3.15**
    s.98(2)(b), **3.27**
    s.230(3), **4.2**
    s.230(4), **4.2**
    s.230(5), **4.2**
Employment Tribunals Act 1996,
    s.21(ge), **6.46**
Equal Pay Act 1970, **Introduction**
Equality Act 2010, **Introduction, 4.2, 4.5, 4.7**
    s.4, **2.2**
    s.9, **2.4**
    s.9(1), **7.6**
    s.9(1)(2), **2.12.1**
    s.9(3), **2.4**
    s.9(4), **2.5**
    s.9(5), **2.12.2**
    s.13, **2.2**
    s.13(5), **2.19**
    s.19, **2.2**
    s.26, **2.2**
    s.27, **2.2**
    s.41, **4.38**
    s.53, **4.39**
    s.83(2)(a), **4.2, 4.38**
    s.108, **4.34**

s.119(4), **6.38**
s.120(1)(a), **4.39**
s.124(3), **6.38**
s.124(4), **6.41**
s.124(5), **6.41**
s.124(6), **6.38**
s.136(2), **6.14**
s.147, **6.23, 6.25.1-3**
s.158, **7.9**
s.159(1)-(4), **7.10**
s.159(5), **7.11**
s.159(6), **7.12**

Equality Act 2010 Explanatory Note 15, **4.37**
Extension of Public Order Act 1936, **1.8**
Modern Slavery Act 2015
    s.8, **2.9.2**
National Minimum Wage Act 1998,
    s.54, **4.2**
Public Order Act, 1936, s.5, **1.6**
Race Relations Act 1965, **Introduction, 1.8**
    ss1-8, **1.8**
Race Relations Act 1968, **Introduction, 1.10, 1.11**
Race Relations Act 1976, **Introduction**
    s.1, **4.11**
    s.71(1), **Introduction**
Race Relations (Amendment) Act 2000, **Introduction**
Sex Disqualification Act 1919, **Introduction**
Sex Discrimination Act 1975, **Introduction**

Rules

Employment Appeal Tribunal Rules 1993, **9.3**
    r.2A, **6.2**

r.3(3)(a), **6.46**

Regulations
Employment Tribunals (Constitution & Rules of Procedure) Regulations 2013,
- r.2, **6.2**
- r.3, **6.17**
- r.39, **6.9**
- r.61(1), **6.37**
- r.62(3), **6.37**
- r.70, **6.46**
- r.71, **6.46**

Working Time Regulations 1998,
- reg2(1), **4.2**

Codes of Practice and Guides
ACAS Code of Practice on Disciplinary and Grievance Procedures (March 2015), **pp89-92**, para:
- 2, **3.11**
- 4, **3.11**
- 24, **3.28**
- 27, **3.8**
- 37, **3.20**
- 43, **3.8**

ACAS Guide to Discipline and Grievances at work (July 2020), **6.18**

Equality Act 2010 Code of Practice (2011), para:
- 2.38, **2.10**
- 2.43, **2.10**
- 2.45, **2.10**
- 2.47, **2.5**
- 4.5, **2.27**

    7.7, **4.24**
    7.8, **2.33**
    9.8, **4.30**
    10.51, **4.36**
    10.52, **4.36**
    12.10, **7.8**
    12.16, **7.10**

Presidential Guidance - Employment Tribunal awards for injury to feelings and psychiatric injury following *De Souza v Vinci Construction (UK) Ltd [2017] EWCA Civ 879*, 26 March 2021, **6.42**

Practice Direction

Practice Direction (Employment Appeal Tribunal - Procedure) 2018,
    PD2.1, **6.46**
    PD2.2, **6.46**

European Treaty and Directives

EC Burden of Proof Directive 97/80, Art. 6, **2.24**
Equal Pay Directive of 1975, **Introduction**
Equal Treatment Directive 1976, **Introduction**
European Union Council Directive 2000/43/EC, **Introduction**
Treaty of Rome 1957, **Introduction**

PREFACE TO FIRST EDITION

After many years of practising as an employment law barrister, I have sought to encapsulate some of that experience in print, simply put in black and white, that I hope will be of assistance to many, be it an employee – current and former, employer, worker, claimant, respondent, HR, student and, of course, the intrigued. This book introduces the race relations laws in Britain as pertaining to employment. It does not seek to cover every minutiae of this fascinating and intriguing subject; it would take a much larger book to achieve that aim successfully.

I have boldly attempted to state where I believe it all began. I accept that some, if not many, would disagree with my starting position. But after spending many weeks researching and reading Hansard at my Inns of Court library (the old-fashioned way i.e. without the benefit of an Internet search engine), I reached the conclusion that 12 June 1956 was as good a starting point as any, which I detail in Chapter One (How It All Began). It saddens me somewhat to see that much of what was discussed over 60 years ago with regards to race relations would not look entirely out of place in some discussions taking place in 2021. In Chapter Two (Equality Act 2010), I discuss the various concepts under the Equality Act 2010 with which one should become familiar to understand conducts deemed to be unlawful. In Chapter Three (Grievance & Disciplinary), I discuss Grievance and Disciplinary procedures and processes. In Chapter Four (Employment Tribunal I), I discuss the Employment Tribunal process, focusing on direct discrimination, indirect discrimination, harassment and victimisation. In Chapter Five (Pleadings), I extend the concepts discussed in Chapter Four by looking at pleadings, the practical and technical side of bringing and defending a claim. I give examples under each of the four heads of claim by referring to scenarios, covering, amongst other things, pleadings and witness statements. In Chapter Six (Employment Tribunal II), I return to the Employment Tribunal, building on matters discussed in Chapter Four. In Chapter Seven (Diversity Awareness & Inclusion) I deal with diversity awareness and inclusion. In Chapter Eight (Training), I deal with training accompanied by questions on matters discussed and raised in this book. In Chapter Nine (Statutes, Rules, Regulations & Links), for ease of reference, I have cited key parts of relevant statutes, rules and regulations covered and discussed in the book together with links to some websites of interest.

Finally, this book and its contents are not a substitution for specific legal advice. If the reader is faced with an issue covered in this book, they should and are strongly advised to seek specific legal advice accordingly. Hopefully, the reason you are reading this part is because you are already either fascinated or intrigued by this area of law. I hope therefore that this book will whet your appetite even more, thus leading to further studies and, if desired to do so, to contribute to improving race relations in the United Kingdom.

PREFACE TO SECOND EDITION

Much has happened since I wrote the last word of the First Edition. In the First Edition I omitted to mention the concept of 'institutional racism.' It was a conscious decision. However, it was unavoidable in this edition for two main reasons. Firstly, professionally, I became part of an issue that was to occupy the sports media (and still does). Second, it has been in the media generally. In consequence, I have written a new Chapter Eight on Institutional Racism. For professional reasons, which is already in the public domain, I declare that I represented three of those involved in the Yorkshire Cricket Club matter that I write about in Chapter Eight.[1] Those three are also now good friends of mine. For that reason, to avoid any allegations of bias, I have fully referenced all that I have written on the matter and have not written anything on the issue that was not or is not already in the public domain. Furthermore, for professional reasons I have expressed no view beyond addressing the concept and complexity of institution racism. Professionally, I should declare that in February 2022 I was in attendance with one of my clients in a meeting with Mr. Julian Knight MP, chair of the digital, culture, media and sport committee on 16 November 2021, and Mr. Alex Sobel MP, via Zoom that was referred to in the Times Newspaper article written about my client by the former England Cricket captain and the highly respected chief cricket reporter, Mr. Michael Atherton.[2]

---

[1] https://www.yorkshirepost.co.uk/sport/cricket/yorkshire-ccc-agree-out-of-court-deal-with-ian-fisher-one-of-staff-members-sacked-in-azeem-rafiq-scandal-3835428

[2] https://www.thetimes.co.uk/article/kunwar-bansil-i-loved-yorkshire-but-i-was-brutally-axed-why-wont-they-listen-to-me-jc6z780n7. See also

Then there was the, "No, but where do you really come from, where do your people come from?" question by Lady Susan Hussey to Ms. Ngozi Fulani, a black British woman and founder of the charity Sistah Space, at Buckingham Palace on 29 November 2022, during a reception on gender-based violence. This question was put to Ms. Fulani despite her having already confirmed to Lady Hussey that, "I am born here and am British." I use the same script but with different actors in Chapter Nine.

Lastly, I have included recent case law to assist the reader and, I am sure you will be pleased to read, I have added only 11 more questions to the previous 60 questions from the First Edition. I promise, they shall be no more in future editions. I hope. May be!

---

https://www.yorkshirepost.co.uk/sport/cricket/yorkshire-ccc-racism-scandal-not-the-black-and-white-issue-many-want-chris-waters-3795983

INTRODUCTION

Friday, 1 October 2021 marks 11 years since the Equality Act 2010 came into force on Friday, 1 October 2010.[3] The 2010 Act brought to an end, in name only, a line of significant and, at times, ground-breaking Race Relations Acts, being the 1965, 1968, 1976 and 2000 (Amendment). All made their mark in the history of race relations legislation in Britain (the equality laws, as applied specifically to Northern Ireland, where they are not contained in a single Act, are beyond the scope of this book).[4] Each grew organically from its predecessor. However, the 1976 Act, which was amended on numerous occasions, including quite significantly by the 2000 (Amendment) Act itself, lasted the test of time until it was repealed 34 years later by the 2010 Act.

On 30 November 2000 the Race Relations (Amendment) Bill received its Royal Assent to become the Race Relations (Amendment) Act 2000 ("the 2000 Act"). The 2000 Act amended the Race Relations Act 1976 – as previously amended – and marked a new landmark in the battle against race discrimination in Britain. Although the pivotal Race Relations Act 1976, which came into force on 22 November 1976, was preceded by two other named domestic legislations repealed by and amalgamated into the 2010 Act, the 1976 Act was the first standalone domestic anti-discriminatory legislation in Britain.

---

[3] https://www.legislation.gov.uk/ukpga/2010/15/contents
[4] The Act forms part of the law of England and Wales. It also, with some exceptions, forms part of the law of Scotland. There are also a few provisions which form part of the law of Northern Ireland.

Although the United Kingdom ceased to be a member of the European Union (EU) on 31 January 2020, implemented on 31 December 2020, the following is nonetheless helpful. On 1 January 1973 the United Kingdom joined the European Economic Community, the predecessor of the EU. From the Treaty of Rome 1957 came the Equal Pay Directive of 1975 and the Equal Treatment Directive of 1976. These Directives, which have their roots in EU law, formed the basis of the Equal Pay Act 1970, which came into force only in December 1975 (EPA 1970), and the Sex Discrimination Act 1975 (SDA 1975).

However, not only did the first race relations legislation not emanate from EU law, but it had already been enacted a decade earlier. In fact, both the race relations Acts of 1965 and 1968 were laws before the EPA 1970 and SDA 1975 came into force. Therefore, not to diminish in any way the impact and importance of the Sex Disqualification Removal Act 1919,[5] one could argue that 'race' was the first characteristic to be 'protected' under domestic legislation; sex (1975), disability (1995), sexual orientation (2003), religion or belief (2003), age (2003) etc. However, it was not until the Race Relations Act 1976 mirrored the SDA 1975 did uniformity of language pertaining to the other anti-discriminatory laws such as Disability Discrimination Act 1995[6], and the Employment Equality Regulations 2003 for sexual orientation, religion or belief, and age, for example, begin to take a form with which we are more familiar today.

---

[5] https://www.gov.uk/government/news/the-sex-disqualification-removal-act-1919
[6] https://www.legislation.gov.uk/ukpga/1995/50/contents

Notably, amongst other things, the amended Race Relations Act 1976 extended to the police and other public authorities. After much political debate,[7] there was now a general statutory duty on specified authorities when carrying out their functions to have due regard to the need to eliminate unlawful racial discrimination and to promote equality of opportunity and good relations between persons of different racial groups.[8] The latter described as, "a positive statutory duty," was to ensure that all such authorities, "not only react to people who test their racial equality policies, but accept that promoting racial equality is a public benefit and is good service and employment practice."[9] As you

---

[7] For example, Lord Lester of Herne Hill's criticism of the Government's initial failure to include positive duties on Public Authorities in the Race Relations (Amendment) Bill: "The United Kingdom has been criticised by the UN Human Rights Committee for not taking steps with sufficient vigour, and by the UN Committee on the Elimination of Racial Discrimination as recently as 1997. It criticised the United Kingdom for the lack of a similar positive legal duty on bodies working in the fields of health, education, social services, planning and housing as that which applied to local authorities. So we stand condemned by two respected international human rights bodies in the race discrimination field. I do not use emotive or exaggerated language. I simply say that it is unacceptable for the United Kingdom to be pilloried in that way because of the refusal by consecutive governments to take effective action. The time is right. There is no reason why that duty cannot be included in this Bill any more than in the Greater London Authority Act, or in the Northern Ireland Act." **House of Lords, Committee Stage**, *Hansard HL, 11 January 2000, col. 788*. On 27 January 2000, Lord Bassam of Brighton announced in the House of Lords that such positive duties would be included in the Bill: **House of Lords, Report Stage**, *Hansard HL, 27 January 2000, col. 1673*

[8] s71(1) of the Race Relations Act 1976, as amended. See also Article 5 of European Union Council Directive 2000/43/EC, to be implemented by 19 July 2003, which states "with a view to ensuring full equality in practice, the principle of equal treatment shall not prevent any Member State from maintaining or adopting specific measures to prevent or compensate for disadvantages linked to racial or ethnic origin."

will see, all this is a far cry from the days when some advocated its – a race relations Act – superfluity.

The Equality Act 2010 replaced the anti-discrimination laws in Britain, amongst other things, 'to reform and harmonise equality law and restate the greater part of the enactments relating to discrimination and harassment related to certain personal characteristics; to prohibit victimisation in certain circumstances; to require the exercise of certain functions to be with regard to the need to eliminate discrimination and other prohibited conduct; to enable duties to be imposed in relation to the exercise of public procurement functions; to increase equality of opportunity.'[10] In consequence, the Equality Act 2010 became the first amalgamated single Act of Britain's anti-discrimination laws.

---

[9] Simon Hughes MP, **House of Commons**, **Standing Committee Stage**, *Hansard HC, Standing Committee D, 2 May 2000 (afternoon)*
[10] Introduction to the Equality Act 2010
(https://www.legislation.gov.uk/ukpga/2010/15/introduction)

~ CHAPTER ONE ~

"The law is the primary factor. The individual is caught in its grip from the earliest stage in life and his moral ideas are developed under its influence."

Professor Karl Olivecrona[11]

---

[11] Taken from his book, *law as fact* (1939), (London: Oxford University Press), p156

HOW IT ALL BEGAN

1.1 There is no consensus as to the "correct" place to start when considering the birth of race relations in Britain. Each writer would have their preferable place at which to begin. I have chosen the date and place as 12 June 1956 at the House of Commons when the then Labour Member of Parliament for Eton and Slough, Mr Archibold Fenner Brockway, the son of a Christian missionary, sought leave of the House to introduce his Private Member's Bill, supported by just eleven other named MPs, among them Mrs Castle and Mr Benn, "to make illegal discrimination to the detriment of any person on the grounds of colour, race and religion in the United Kingdom."

House of Commons, First Reading
Hansard HC, 12 June 1956, col.247, 248
Mr A. Fenner Brockway

> It is very difficult to estimate opinion on this matter. There are under-currents of feeling, it may even be in the subconscious, which will respond under favourable conditions towards, or retreat under unfavourable conditions from, racial equality. But, Sir, I would say that broadly speaking the British people recognise that identity as human beings is greater than differences of race, colour or religion…I recognise that there must be a limitation of the powers of legislation. Often acts of discrimination are due to prejudice, to ignorance or to irrational repulsion, and those can be removed only by education or experience.

1.2   In total, Mr Brockway made some nine attempts to make various forms of race discrimination unlawful; each failing to make its way onto the statute books. Some were quite vociferous in their opposition to such a Bill. Take, for example, the views of the Member of Parliament for Buckinghamshire, South, Mr Ronald Bell, during the Second reading of Mr Brockway's second attempt.

House of Commons, Second Reading
Hansard HC, 10 May 1957, col. 1426,1427
Mr Ronald Bell

> It is a wholly deplorable Measure. The hon. Member for Eton and Slough [Mr Brockway] holds strong views about the treatment of coloured people, and he is quite entitled to hold those views. Indeed, my strongest feeling in approaching the subject is that everybody is entitled to have his own views about it. I am very sorry to see any attempt made by legislation to try to stop that and to ram the views of the hon. Member for Eton and Slough by Statute down the throats of other people. It is quite easy for those who take an interest in particular aspects of the matter of the treatment of coloured peoples to build up for themselves and in the minds of others a belief that there is something specific, definable and wicked in a colour bar. It may be that in some parts of the world there is something so definable and specific, but this Bill relates to the United Kingdom, and there is certainly nothing of that kind in this country.

House of Commons, Second Reading
Hansard HC, 24 May 1957, col. 1603
Mr Bernard Braine

> This is a matter which goes to the very root of human relationships. Try as hard as we can, we cannot compel people to love one another, we cannot compel people to ignore differences to which they attach importance, any more than we can ignore the fact that some people talk more loudly, take fewer baths, wear dirtier clothes, or have more unpleasant habits, than others. This is something which is absolutely fundamental. Where racial prejudice does exists – and unhappily it does exist in our midst – it calls for education, sympathy and knowledge, but it certainly does not call for legislation.

House of Commons, First Reading
Bill to make it illegal to refuse admission to lodging houses, restaurants, dance halls, and similar establishments on the grounds of race
Hansard HC, 8 July 1958, col. 207
Mr John Baird

> At some time in the near future, it may be necessary to pass legislation restricting immigration to this country, but if we make such legislation it must not be on the basis of colour. But even restricted immigration will not solve the problem, and we certainly will not solve it by segregation. In the long run, the only way to solve it will be by education among both races, and by seeing that much more welfare work is carried out among coloured people. Some people argue that we shall not do anything by legislation; that we can solve this problem only by education. That may have been

true some time ago, but there are so many cases of this kind arising now that I say that legislation and education must go hand-in-hand.

1.3 The introduction of Mr Brockway's fourth Bill in the Commons on 12 November 1958 followed a summer of, "race clashes," in Nottingham and Notting Hill Gate. The riots "are commonly seen as an important watershed in the development of racialised politics in Britain. It is certainly true that the events in these two localities helped bring to national prominence issues which had previously been discussed only locally or within government departments."[12] The National Council for Liberties was reported to have been appalled at the continued racial clashes, stating that, "examples in one area are being copied in other areas and unless speedily checked by public opinion will clearly increase and spread."

The Times, 3 September 1958, p7

There had been a complete lack of leadership "on the evil of colour bar and race discrimination…If the Government-subsidised British Travel and Holidays Association had never allowed hotels which refuse accommodation to coloured people to appear on its list, if magistrates had exercised their powers under the law to refuse to renew licences of public houses which discriminate against coloured people, if the local administration had refused licences to dance halls which

---

[12] Solomos, J. (1993) *Race and racism in Britain*, 2nd Ed., (London: Macmillan), pp59-60

impose a colour bar, and people in authority were given a lead in the fight against discrimination instead of in many cases tacitly condoning it, then this kind of thing would not have happened." The council called upon political parties, local authorities, and magistrates "to take all action which will discourage discrimination" and urged leaders of the Churches, the trade union movement, and all in positions of influence to make a public stand against discrimination.

1.4 Tragically, on 17 May 1959, Mr Kelso Cochrane, an Antiguan living in Notting Hill, was alleged to have been involved in a fight with some white youths in which he was fatally stabbed. Despite the obvious concerns by some sectors there still appeared to exist a degree of caution amongst politicians as to whether legislation prohibiting racial discrimination would be effective.

House of Commons
Hansard HC, 4 June 1959, col. 368
Mr Fisher

> To ask the Secretary of State for the Home Department whether, in view of the recent murder of a West Indian in the streets of Notting Hill and of attacks upon the property of coloured residents in that area, he will issue a public statement deploring such manifestations of colour prejudice and violence…

House of Commons
Hansard HC, 4 June 1959, col. 369
The Secretary of State for the Home Department and Lord Privy Seal (Mr R.A. Butler)

> Racial discrimination has no place in our law and responsible opinion everywhere will unhesitatingly condemn any attempt to forment it.

House of Commons
Hansard HC, 4 June 1959, col. 371
Mr S. Silverman

> Will the right hon. Gentleman bear in mind that while it is perfectly true, as he said, that racial discrimination forms no part of our law, there is nothing in our law to make racial discrimination itself illegal? Does he not think that the time is rapidly approaching when there ought to be?

House of Commons
Hansard HC, 4 June 1959, col. 371
The Secretary of State for the Home Department and Lord Privy Seal (Mr R.A. Butler)

> Part of what I said was that it was not known in our law, and perhaps deliberately to take action against it might not be so effective as the hon. Member might think. That is why I do not want to step into that part without a great deal more consideration.

1.5 In 1964 Mr Brockway again sought leave of the Commons to introduce his revised Bill. This time he seemed to sense a sea of change in attitudes amongst his peers towards the need for some kind of race relations legislation to deal with the various allegations of racial discrimination that were being made. This was no more noticeable than when he sought leave of the House to introduce what turned out to be his final attempt to have his Bill enacted.

House of Commons, First Reading
Hansard HC, 14 January 1964, col. 42,45
Mr A. Fenner Brockway

This is the ninth occasion when I have introduced a Bill dealing with racial discrimination. This has not been an academic exercise; it has been a progressive process. Each year support for a Measure on this subject has grown. When I first introduced a Bill ten years ago, I could obtain as sponsors only some of my hon. Friends on the back benches. Today, if the House gives permission for the Bill to be introduced, the list of sponsors will show that the Bill has the support of the Front Bench of the Labour Party, the Liberal Party and many hon. Members opposite. I hope that the Bill will pass during the present Parliament, but I am quite confident that on the tenth occasion of introducing it, in the new Parliament, it will not only have the opportunity to be considered but will have a majority in the House…It is said that legislation cannot cure the evils of race discrimination. It cannot; but in public places and in public expression the law can give a lead…Much of the world is moving forward to a recognition that racial demarcation is a betrayal of the human family. I ask the House: is this country, whose great pride is democratic tolerance, to be left behind?

1.6 In October 1964 Labour defeated the Conservatives and the Liberals in the General Election by 317 seats to 304 and 9 seats, respectively, to form the next British government. However, there was to be no "tenth occasion" for Mr Brockway, as he lost his seat and, consequently, was not amongst the elected Labour MPs, although he was offered and accepted a life peerage. But, all was not lost. On 7 April 1965 Sir Frank Soskice introduced to the Commons a Bill to prohibit discrimination on racial grounds in places of public resort; to prevent the enforcement or imposition on racial grounds of restrictions on the transfer of tenancies; to penalise incitement to racial hatred; and to amend s5 of the Public Order Act 1936.[13]

House of Commons, Second Reading
Hansard HC, 3 May 1965, col. 926
Sir Frank Soskice

> To form a judgment on this Bill, it is essential to understand why the Government have thought it in the public interest to introduce it and what it is designed to achieve...It would be a tragedy of the first order if our country, with its unrivalled tradition of tolerance and fair

---

[13] Section 7 of the 1965 Act – Extension of Public Order Act 1936, s5 to written matter:

For section 5 of the Public Order Act, 1936, there shall be substituted the following section:

"Any person who in any public place or at any public meeting –
(a) uses threatening, abusive or insulting words or behaviour, or
(b) distributes or displays any writing, sign or visible representation which is threatening, abusive or insulting, with intent to provoke a breach of the peace or whereby a breach of the peace is likely to be occasioned, shall be guilty of an offence."

play as between one man or woman and another and perfect respect for the rights and personal worth and dignity of the individual, should see the beginnings of the development of a distinction between first and second class citizens and the disfigurement which can arise from inequality of treatment and incitement to feelings of hatred directed to the origins of particular citizens, something for which they are not responsible.

House of Commons, Second Reading
Hansard HC, 3 May 1965, col. 1049,1050
Sir Dingle Foot

Before closing, I should like to make one word of personal acknowledgement in which I feel that all my hon. Friends on this side, and, indeed, some hon. Members opposite, would wish to join. This Measure was clearly foreshadowed in our election manifesto, but…it owes its inspiration in particular to one man, Fenner Brockway. He has done more than any man I know, in this House or outside to promote understanding between different races and between different members of the Commonwealth. I deeply regret, as will many others, that he is not here to take part in this debate tonight, although the Bill will reach him in another place. It is, however, a matter of very great personal pride and satisfaction to me that on this occasion I should inherit his mantle. It is for those reasons that I commend the Bill to the House.

House of Lords, Second Reading
Hansard HL, 26 July 1965, col. 1006
Lord Stoneham

I think your Lordships will agree that it is almost impossible to approach this subject without acknowledging the very great work done in this field over the years by my noble friend Lord Brockway. It is many years since, in another place, he first introduced a Private Member's Bill aimed at outlawing racial discrimination. He was not successful then; nor was he in the many years when he tried to do the same thing. But I am quite sure that we all agree that he has made a great contribution. He has helped bring us to the point at which we are now...

1.7 On 8 November 1965, as predicted by Mr Brockway – albeit not *his* Bill – on 14 January 1964, the Bill described by Sir Dingle Foot as "a landmark in our legislation" received its Royal Assent and thus became the first race relations legislation in Britain; the Race Relations Act 1965.

1.8 The Race Relations Act 1965 consisted of just eight sections and one schedule.[14] Among other things, it made it unlawful for any person, being the proprietor or manager of or employed for the purposes of any place of public resort [...], to practise discrimination on the ground of colour, race, or ethnic or national origins against persons seeking access to or facilities or services at that place.[15] Also, the

---

[14] Discrimination in places of public resort: s1; The Race Relations Board and conciliation committees: s2; Proceedings for enforcement of section 1 in England and Wales: s3; Proceedings for enforcement of section 1 in Scotland: s4; Discriminatory restrictions on disposal of tenancies: s5; Incitement to racial hatred: s6; Extension of Public Order Act, 1936, s. 5 to written matter: s7; Short title, commencement and extent: s8; Schedule: Provisions as to Race Relations Board and Local Conciliation Committees.
[15] s1 of the Race Relations Act 1965

1965 Act established the Race Relations Board[16] to, among other things, help secure compliance with s1 of the 1965 Act and at such times as the Secretary of State directed, make annual reports to him with respect to the exercise of its or its local conciliation committees. The Secretary of State would lay such report before Parliament; a function that remains with us, today. Proceedings in England and Wales, whether criminal or civil, were brought, solely, by the Attorney General. The 1965 Act was generally deemed by many as a success but failed to prevent discrimination in areas where some thought it should, such as, for example, those pertaining to employment. The second annual report of the Race Relations Board classified the total of 690 complaints it received during the period of 1 April 1967 and 31 March 1968 into 108 covered by existing legislation. The Board was unable to investigate 574 of the complaints, since they fell outside its present powers. Of these, the bulk, 254 (44%), were about employment and 61(11.6%) were about housing.[17] Due to its shortfalls, some called for the 1965 Act to be extended to areas such as employment and housing. Therefore, on 8 April 1968 Mr Callaghan presented a Bill to the Commons to make fresh provisions with respect to discrimination on racial grounds, and to make provision with respect to relations with people of different origins.

---

[16] s2 of the Race Relations Act 1965
[17] Hansard, vol. 763, col. 133

House of Commons, Second Reading
Hansard HC, 23 April 1968, col. 53
Mr James Callaghan

> The House has rarely faced an issue of greater social significance for our country and our children. We are discussing a subject which is heavily charged with emotion, in which there is nothing easier than to fan the flames of suspicion and resentment or of fear…This is a time for responsibility, for leadership and, if I may dare to use the word, for nobility. My starting point is that society is most healthy and most free from tension when it is based on the simple principle that every citizen within its boundaries shares equally in the same freedoms, the same responsibilities, the same opportunities and the same benefits. The history of the British people is a story of struggle to achieve full citizenship in our own country. It would be a denial of our own history if, having won these freedoms for ourselves, we were now to exclude other groups who have come to live here as full citizens. None of us can shrink from the challenge of racialism. It is a live force in this country, but I believe that it is not yet deep rooted, and this Bill puts to the test what our response is to be. Legislation, of course, cannot stand alone. I have frequently said that it needs to be supported by effective social policies, but, on the other hand, social policies by themselves will not be sufficient without legislation.

1.9 Despite its limitations, the very existence of the 1965 Act was attributed as a major factor towards reducing racial discrimination in Britain.

House of Commons, Second Reading
Hansard HC, 23 April 1968, col. 55
Mr James Callaghan

It is clear from the evidence of the Race Relations Board in its annual Report, and from other quarters, that legislation has proved of value in the limited field to which the 1965 Act applied. Let me quote from paragraph 22 of the Report, on the more declaratory aspect of that law:

> *"The mere passage of the law probably decreased the incidence of discrimination."*

Again, in paragraph 26:

> *"The Board is satisfied that conciliation would have been virtually impossible were it not for the sanctions provided in the Act."*

There is also the evidence from the United States that the very declaration of what the law is tends to lessen discrimination in practice. Mr Anthony Lewis, the chief correspondent in London of the *New York Times*, wrote in the London *Times* yesterday, referring to the United States:

> *"…the legislation works because most people in our two countries are basically law abiding and will adjust to a changed legal framework."*

I attach great importance to the declaratory nature of the first part of the Bill. I believe that what Mr Lewis said is profoundly true, and that the very process of giving the law brings an instinctive response from the great majority of our citizens.

Sir Dingle Foot also drew from the American experience.

House of Commons, Second Reading
Hansard HC, 23 April 1968, col. 83,84
Sir Dingle Foot

> …the question we must consider when we are thinking about the racial discrimination which undoubtedly exists at present is whether the climate can be altered in some degree by legislation…Here we are dealing with discrimination, and I suggest…that we cannot ignore the American experience. We know the events that have taken place in the United States during the past few weeks. In that kind of situation there are not only differences of race and colour but social differences which coincide. The Street Report, to which the right hon. and learned Gentleman referred, seems to me to contain the most convincing evidence as to what can be achieved by legislation. On page 41 it refers to changes in the attitude of industry, and states:
>
>> *"Further evidence of changes in public opinion which can be directly related to legislation is to be found by examining changes in the attitudes of industry, the unions and other bodies towards legislation. When a bill was introduced by the Massachusetts legislature to outlaw employment discrimination in 1945, it was fiercely opposed by industry, the unions, the churches, the legal profession and other groups, on the grounds that it would interfere with freedom of choice, and would ultimately increase prejudice. In*

time the law ceased to be opposed, and on the contrary, industry began to develop its own schemes to co-operate with the commission and to further its aims. This pattern of opposition followed by acceptance and then active co-operation was reproduced in many States. The final stage is exemplified on a national scale by 'Plans for Progress' and by the vigorous support given by the leaders of trade unions to the introduction of Title VII of the Federal Civil Rights Act, 1964."[18]

That was the experience in the United States, and the result described there would not have been brought about without legislation.

1.10 Due to its relative novelty, the debates on the Bill to the 1968 Act were, arguably, the liveliest and widest of the race relations' debates. Mr Reginald Maudling described the above debate "as befits the subject, this has been a very grave debate, and one of the best that I have ever heard in the House. It is well that it should be so."[19] The Bill received its Royal Assent on 25 October 1968. The 1968 Act consisted of 29 sections and 4 schedules contained within three parts. Race relations legislation in Britain had grown. For the purposes of the 1968 Act, a person discriminated against another if on the ground of colour, race or ethnic or national origins they treated that other, in any situation to which s2 (provision of goods, facilities and services), s3 (Employment), s4 (Trade unions, and

---

[18] See volume 42 of the United States Code, beginning at section 2000e. Title VII prohibits employment discrimination based on race, colour, religion, sex and national origin

[19] House of Commons, Second Reading. Hansard HC, 23 April 1968, col. 147

employers' and trade organisations) or s5 (Housing accommodation, and business and other premises) applied, less favourably than they treated or would have treated other persons. Pertaining to employment Mr Callaghan said:

House of Commons, Second Reading
Hansard HC, 23 April 1968, col. 56,57
Mr James Callaghan

> There are some encouraging signs that coloured people are being accepted in industry on their merits; but on the evidence it is abundantly clear that coloured people are handicapped in their search for work despite their qualifications. Some of them are refused the promotion to more responsible posts to which their qualifications entitle them. Perhaps some of the first generation immigrants are resigned to this. But there will be growing tension if coloured youngsters leaving school in the next few years cannot readily get jobs for which they are qualified on the same terms as their white contemporaries. There is evidence that this is happening now; and these are the children who are, and who will be, the product of our own education system, brought up in our own traditions. It hardly needs me to underline the danger to our society if intelligent, high-spirited young people are marked down as second-class citizens because of their colour.

1.11   On 17 February 1976 Mr Roy Jenkins introduced a Bill that was to form the basis of the Race Relations Act 1976. As with its predecessors the Bill was to make fresh provision with respect to discrimination etc.

House of Commons, Second Reading
Hansard HC, 4 March 1976, col. 1547-1552
The Secretary of State for the Home Department and Lord Privy Seal (Mr Roy Jenkins)

A great deal has changed in the decade since the introduction of the first Race Relations Bill in 1965. The character of Britain's coloured population has altered dramatically. Ten years ago, less than one-quarter of the coloured population was born in Britain. More than three out of every four coloured people were immigrants, a substantial number of them fairly recent arrivals. By contrast, today about two out of every five of the coloured population have been born here, and the time is not far off when the majority of the coloured population will be British-born.

The first principle upon which the Government's policy is based is the clear recognition that the vast majority of the coloured population will remain permanently in this country, and that a substantial and increasing proportion of that population belongs to our country in the fullest sense of being born and educated here as fellow citizens. The second principle is that the members of Britain's racial minorities are entitled to full and equal treatment regardless of their colour, race or national origins. Racial discrimination and the disadvantages experienced by sections of the community are morally repugnant to a civilised and democratic society. These evils are also a form of economic and social waste which a society with any sense of enlightened and far-sighted self-interest cannot afford. They are a source of individual injustices for which there should be effective legal remedies...The fourth principle is that, although effective legislation against racial discrimination is a necessary condition of equal opportunity and good race relations, it is not in itself a sufficient or complete condition. The success of legislation depends on the one hand upon the leadership of Government and Parliament and on the other hand upon the response of society as a whole...Action is, therefore, needed to tackle racial disadvantages as well as discrimination.

We now have behind us the experience of 10 years of the working of the present legislation. I am not too much impressed by those who harp continually on the weaknesses and imperfections of the Acts of 1965 and 1968. Of course, those imperfections exist. It would, indeed, have been surprising if they had been perfect in every detail for dealing with a new and unfamiliar problem for our country. It is interesting to observe that even in the United States of America, which has much longer experience of the problems of racial segregation and discrimination, Congress found it necessary in 1972 to make important improvements in the civil rights legislation enacted some eight years earlier. By coincidence, the same period of eight years has elapsed between the introduction of the Race Relations Act 1968 and today's Bill...Yet at the end of this decade, which stretches back to 1965, despite all our efforts both statutory bodies have forcibly drawn attention, as they should, to the inability of existing legislation to deal with widespread patterns of discrimination, especially in employment and housing, to a lack of confidence among minority groups in the utility of the law...

The Bill makes several important changes in the definition of "discrimination"...The Bill covers not only deliberate and direct discrimination on racial grounds but also unjustifiable indirect discrimination.

1.12 On 22 November 1976 the Race Relations Act 1976 received its Royal Assent. The new Act had some 80 sections and 5 schedules, spanning ten parts. The 1976 Act had been amended at various times since it was enacted and was the major race relations legislation in Britain until it was repealed in 2010. However, each of the major Acts helped form the foundation for the next and, arguably, each influencing the "moral ideas" of the British public upon which to build the next piece of legislation until such laws were, ideally, deemed surplus to requirements. "It is a pity," said Mr Maudling during the Second reading of the Race Relations Bill, "that a Bill of this character should be thought necessary. In a sense, it is a human failure that it should be necessary to proceed by legislation in these matters. Compulsion should not be necessary to ensure that men and women live happily together and treat one another in a decent and civilised manner."[20]

1.13 Undoubtedly, race relations legislation in Britain has come a long way since the 1965 Act. Changing attitudes have led to some attempting not only to eliminate the "act" of

---

[20] House of Commons, Second Reading. Hansard HC, 23 April 1968, col. 147

discrimination on the grounds of race but also the "ideology" of racism. The tragic death of Mr Cochrane in 1959 was reported and led only to a few questions being raised in Parliament. Thirty-four years later the tragic death of a young black man, Stephen Lawrence, led not only to mass public outcry but on 31 July 1997 to the commissioning of a report headed by Sir William Macpherson of Cluny. The Macpherson Inquiry looked into matters arising from the death of Stephen, in order particularly to identify the lessons to be learned from the investigation and prosecution of racially motivated crimes.

1.14 On 15 February 1999 the Macpherson report was delivered to the Home Secretary, among other things, making 70 recommendations to the Government. Recommendation 11 stated that:

That the full force of the Race Relations legislation should apply to all police officers, and that Chief Officers of Police should be made vicariously liable for the acts and omissions of their officers relevant to that legislation.[21]

1.15 Some were surprised when the then Home Secretary, Mr Jack Straw, indicated that he would adopt Recommendation 11 in its entirety, covering not only the police, but also other public authorities such as the civil service and the immigration service.

---

[21] The extension of the Race Relations Act to all public services, and the extension of vicarious liability to the police, were among the proposals in the Commission for Racial Equality's Third Review of the 1976 Act

1.16 On 8 April 2010, precisely 42 years to the date when, due to the shortcomings in the Race Relations Act 1965, on 8 April 1968 Mr Callaghan presented a Bill that would later form the basis of the Race Relations Act 1968 (which contained the first provisions making it unlawful to discriminate in relation to employment on racial grounds), the Equality Bill received its Royal Assent to set in motion the beginning of the end of the last Race Relations Act to bear that name. Along with other equality laws, which included the Sex Discrimination 1975 and the Disability Discrimination 1995 to name a few, the Race Relations Act 1976 was amalgamated into the new all-embracing Equality Act 2010, which came into force on 1 October 2010.

1.17 "The six race relations and equality Acts between 1965 and 2010 have had an impact," contributed Lord Prior of Brampton, the Parliamentary Under-Secretary of State, Department for Business and Industrial Energy, during the "Race in the Workplace: The McGregor-Smith Review," on 24 April 2017. "Overt racism is rarely seen," and concludes, "I hope that in two, three, four or five years' time, we can look back at this as a moment when things started to accelerate. However, I fear that we need some patience."[22]

1.18 In the summer of 2020 British Prime Minister Boris Johnson asked Dr Sewell CBE if he, "would be willing to chair a Commission to investigate race and ethnic disparities in the UK. He felt that the UK needed to consider important questions about the state of race relations today,

---

[22] House of Lords. Hansard HL, 24 April 2017, Vol. 782, col. 1256-1259

and that there needed to be a thorough examination of why so many disparities persist."[23] "We needed to work out what can be done to eliminate or mitigate them," wrote Dr Sewell. He accepted, which led to the Commission on Race and Ethnic Disparities: The Report in March 2021, which concluded, amongst other things, "Put simply we no longer see a Britain where the system is deliberately rigged against ethnic minorities. The impediments and disparities do exist, they are varied, and ironically very few of them are directly to do with racism. Too often 'racism' is the catch-all explanation, and can be simply implicitly accepted rather than explicitly examined."[24] However, it would be an understatement simply to say that the Commission on Race and Ethnic Disparities: The Report has been heavily criticised for much of its findings and conclusions to the point of its being discredited as an unreliable source of work worthy of scholarly citation. In fact, in a question to Baron Berridge on 21 April 2021, Lord Woolley of Woodford asked, "Yesterday the government Minister Kemi Badenoch, […] stated, to my great relief, that no one, not least the Government, is denying institutional racism as distinct from verbal racism. She went on to say that it is not everywhere, and I think we can all agree with that. But the [Commission on Race and Ethnic Disparities: The Report] said, and the Minister confirmed, that Dr Sewell and his

---

[23] "Forward from the Chair" of the Commission on Race and Ethnic Disparities: The Report
(https://assets.publishing.service.gov.uk/government/uploads/system/uploads/attachment_data/file/974507/20210331_-_CRED_Report_-_FINAL_-_Web_Accessible.pdf)
[24] Commission on Race and Ethnic Disparities: The Report, p.8

commissioners did not find systemic racism in this report from the deluge of evidence, including from myself. Given that dramatic but welcome U-turn in acknowledging systemic race inequalities, were the commissioners incompetent or in wilful denial?"[25]

1.19 Among other things, today we have the Black Lives Matter movement and footballers "Taking the Knee," at major sporting events. As recent as July 2021 we have witnessed the racial abuse by some sectors of society aimed at some players of the English national football team, described by Lord Woolley as, "a brilliant team that took a collective stand in taking the knee against the very racism that the black players were subject to after Sunday's defeat,"[26] because they had the misfortune to miss their respective penalties. In a survey of 1212 football fans in Britain conducted between 5-10 August 2021, the fans were asked, "how concerned, if at all, are you about each of the following happening at a football stadium [for the 2021/22] season?" 25% were concerned about personally experiencing racist abuse; 52% were concerned about witnessing another fan receiving racist abuse; and 62% were concerned about witnessing a player receiving racist abuse.[27] This book is about race relations in employment and not about footballers. However, it would not have escaped

---

[25] House of Lords. Hansard HL, 'Commission on Race and Ethnic Disparities," 21 April 2021, Vol. 811, col. 1859

[26] House of Lords. Hansard HL, "Racism in Sport," 13 July 2021, Vol. 813, col. 1712

[27] YouGov/Sky Survey Results (https://docs.cdn.yougov.com/btc4t3y2xt/SkyResults_Racisminfootball_GBsample_August21_w.pdf)

some to notice the relevance to some issues raised in this book. Whether one is a highly paid sports(wo)man or a lower paid worker in comparison, one's place of work (be it at stadia, on shopfloors, in offices, in factories etc.) is not a place that one would be, should be or ought to be expected to accept *any level* of racial abuse, harassment etc.

1.20 Responding to Mr Maudling's comment, during the Second reading of the Race Relations Bill in 1968 over 50 years ago,[28] when and if racial discrimination will be permanently eliminated, ensuring that men and women live happily together and treat one another in a decent and civilised manner remains to be seen, but, sadly, that does not appear to be any time soon.

---

[28] "It is a pity that a Bill of this character should be thought necessary. In a sense, it is a human failure that it should be necessary to proceed by legislation in these matters. Compulsion should not be necessary to ensure that men and women live happily together and treat one another in a decent and civilised manner." House of Commons, Second Reading. Hansard HC, 23 April 1968, col. 147

~ CHAPTER TWO ~

"Moreover, "racial" is not a term of art, either legal or, I surmise, scientific. I apprehend that anthropologists would dispute how far the word "race" is biologically at all relevant to the species amusingly called *homo sapiens*."

Lord Simon of Glaisdale[29]

---

[29] *Ealing London Borough Council v Race Relations Board* [1972] AC 342

EQUALITY ACT 2010

2.1 This chapter deals with the concepts of 'race,' direct discrimination, indirect discrimination, harassment and victimisation.

'Race'

2.2 'Race' is one of the protected characteristics,[30] the relevance of which shall become apparent throughout this book, especially in relation to direct[31] and indirect[32] discrimination, harassment[33] and victimisation[34].

2.3 What is 'race'? Ask a sociologist, biologist and anthropologist and we engage in an entirely different debate to that defined under the Act. One will say there is one race, the human race. One will say there is no race, but a human species. One may even take you back to an 18th Century botanist's four racial groups. Outside the ambit of the Act, 'race' is widely accepted as being a social construct. Likewise, when we refer to 'race' under the Act we are referring *specifically* to a statutory construct, relying on a definition that is found within the Act *itself*. It is important to bear this in mind. A good example of this social and legal construct in operation was given by Dr Steve Jones, during one of his excellent Reith Lectures in 1991 in which he tells

---

[30] s.4 Equality Act 2010
[31] s.13 Equality Act 2010
[32] s.19 Equality Act 2010
[33] s.26 Equality Act 2010
[34] s.27 Equality Act 2010

of the following: "In 1987 a secretary from Virginia sued her employer for discriminating against her because she was black. She lost on the grounds that, as she had red hair, she must be white. She then worked for a black employer and sued him for discriminating against her as she was white. She lost again; the court found that she could not be white as she had been to a black school."[35]

Racial Group

2.4 Under the Act, 'race' includes colour, nationality, ethnic or national origins.[36] A racial group is, 'a group of persons defined by reference to race,' and, 'a person's racial group is a reference to a racial group into which the person falls.'[37] For instance, 'British' people could be a racial group, and although the Scots and English are not racial groups defined by reference to 'ethnic origins,' they could be a racial group with reference to their 'national origins.'[38] Under the Race Relations Act 1976, "racial group" *meant* a group of persons defined by reference to colour, race, nationality or ethnic or national origins, and references to a person's racial group referred to any racial group into which they fell. However, by defining 'race' *itself* as *including* colour, nationality, ethnic or national origins (as opposed to the narrower definition of

---

[35] *Cousins under the Skin* by Dr Steve Jones – The Reith Lectures 1991 (https://www.bbc.co.uk/programmes/p00gxr7d)
[36] s.9 Equality Act 2010
[37] s.9(3) Equality Act 2010
[38] *Northern Joint Police Board (appellants) v Power (respondent)* [1997] IRLR 610

'race' under the 1976 Act), the Act appears to provide a non-exhaustive list.

2.5 Notably, however, even though a racial group has more than one distinct racial group that 'does not prevent it from constituting a particular racial group.'[39] For example, a Grenadian national would be a member of a racial group that comprises of people both who are Grenadians and all foreign nationals. Likewise, 'black Britons' could be members of a racial group that comprises of people who are both black and British. A racial group may have many parts to its form. For example, a 'Nigerian' may be defined by colour, nationality or ethnic or national origin.[40] In a case decided under the Race Relations Act 1976, the then House of Lords held that, "Provided a person who joins the group feels himself or herself to be a member of it, and is accepted by other members, then he is, for the purposes of the Act, a member."[41] Additionally, a person's racial group can be defined in the negative such as non-English, non-Trinidadian etc. In a particular case, the claimant belonged to three racial groups, two of which were framed in the negative, described as, "Cypriot, non-British, and non-EEC."[42]

---

[39] s.9(4) Equality Act 2010
[40] Equality Act 2010 Code of Practice, para. 2.47
[41] *Mandla v Lee* [1983] ICR 385
[42] *Orphanos (Appellant) v. Queen Mary College (Respondents) [1985] IRLR 349*

Ethnicity

2.6 The term 'Ethnicity' is arguably the most misused and misunderstood of the categories of 'race'. A well-informed friend of mine who accused an institution of 'institutional racism,' which attracted much national media attention confessed to me that, until recently, she had no idea what ethnicity was. Another friend of mine stated that two people were of the same ethnicity by reference to colour and being from the same continent, not even the same country! Such misunderstandings and confusion are probably not helped by the continual reference to "ethnic minority" and "minority ethnic" groups because such terms are more symbolic of what is meant than their true meaning. A black person is frequently referred to as an ethnic minority without any reference to their ethnicity. Further confusion lies in who it is that defines a person's ethnicity. For example, a sixth generation English born black person of Ghanaian ancestry may wish to define themselves of both British and Ghanaian ethnicities. The former makes them part of the majority whilst at the same time by way of the latter, being part of the minority. However, currently, it is highly likely that this person would be defined solely as an "ethnic minority" in the eyes on many.

2.7 'Ethnic...origins' means a group that is a segment of the population distinguished from others by a sufficient combination of shared customs, beliefs, traditions and characteristics derived from a common or presumed common past. "For a group to constitute an ethnic group it must regard itself and be regarded by others as a distinct community by virtue of certain characteristics."[43] In a case decided under the Race Relations Act 1976 it was held that Sikhs are an ethnic group, which means that religious and culture factors may also be relevant in defining one's ethnicity. It was held that, "Some of these characteristics are essential; others are not essential but one or more of them will commonly be found and will help to distinguish the group from the surrounding community. The conditions which appear to me to be essential are these: (1) a long-shared history, of which the group is conscious as distinguishing it from other groups, and the memory of which it keeps alive; (2) a cultural tradition of its own, including family and social customs and manners, often but not necessarily associated with religious observance. In addition to those two essential characteristics the following characteristics are, in my opinion, relevant; (3) either a common geographical origin, or descent from a small number of common ancestors; (4) a common language, not necessarily peculiar to the group; (5) a common literature peculiar to the group; (6) a common religion different from that of neighbouring groups or from the general community surrounding it; (7) being a minority or being an oppressed or a dominant group within a larger community."[44]

2.8 However, in another case decided under the Race Relations Act 1976 it was held that direct discrimination, which we deal with below, on grounds of ethnic origins was not limited to discrimination based on membership of an ethnic

---

[43] *Mandla v Lee* [1983] ICR 385, 390
[44] *Mandla v Lee* [1983] ICR 385, 390

group as defined above. It was also held to embrace discrimination on grounds of ethnic origin in the narrower sense i.e. discrimination on the ground of someone else's decent or lineage. In this case, a Jewish faith school applied an admission policy where an applicant child's mother had to be either Jewish by birth or converted to Orthodox Judaism ("the matrilineal test"). The child's mother had converted from being a Roman Catholic to Judaism, 'under the auspices of a non-Orthodox synagogue.' Her conversion was not deemed to be in accordance with Orthodox standards, resulting in the child's admission being refused. It was held that the child had been refused admission on grounds of his ethnic origins and that constituted direct discrimination.

2.9 In any case, although a case of unlawful discrimination because of religion would be brought rightly under the Equality Act 2010 by relying on the protected characteristic of religion or belief, 'Jewish,' can mean a member of a particular ethnic origin as well as a member of a particular religious faith.[45] Rastafarians could not be held to be a separate racial group. Although they are a separate group with identifiable characteristics, they have not established some separate identity by reference to their ethnic origins.[46] Gypsies as a 'wandering race (by themselves called 'Romany'),' are a minority, with a long-shared history and common geographical origin,' are a racial group.[47]

---

[45] *Seide (appellant) v Gillette Industries Ltd (respondents)* [1980] IRLR 427
[46] *Dawkins (appellant) v Department of the Environment sub nom Crown Suppliers PSA (respondents)* [1993] IRLR 284

2.9.1 A person's immigration status was held not to be equated with "nationality" for the purpose of the Equality Act 2010.[48] The claimants entered the UK on domestic workers' visas obtained by their employers. It was found that they had been treated appallingly. "These employees were treated disgracefully, in a way which employees who did not share their vulnerable immigration status would not have been treated. As the employment tribunals found, this was because of the vulnerability associated with their immigration status. The issue for us is a simple one: does discrimination on grounds of immigration status amount to discrimination on grounds of nationality under the 1976 and 2010 Acts?"

2.9.2 In dismissing the claimants' appeals in which they argued that they were treated badly because of their race, the Supreme Court concluded, "…the present law, although it can redress some of those harms, cannot redress them all. Parliament may well wish to address its mind to whether the remedy provided by s.8 of the Modern Slavery Act 2015[49] is too restrictive in its scope and whether an employment tribunal should have jurisdiction to grant some recompense for the ill-treatment meted out to workers such as these,

---

[47] *Commission for Racial Equality (appellants/plaintiffs) v. Dutton (respondent/defendant)* [1989] IRLR 8

[48] *Onu (appellant) v. Akwiwu and another (respondents); Taiwo (appellant) v. Olaigbe and another (respondents)* [2016] IRLR 719; [2016] ICR 756; [2016] UKSC 31

[49] 'Power to make slavery and trafficking reparation orders' [https://www.legislation.gov.uk/ukpga/2015/30/section/8/enacted]

along with the other remedies which it does have power to grant."[50]

Nationality and National Origin

2.10 Importantly, nationality (or citizenship) is the specific legal relationship between a person and a state through birth or naturalisation. National origins must have identifiable elements, both historic and geographic, which at least at some point in time indicate the existence or previous existence of a nation.[51] "A person's own national origin is not something that can be changed, though national origin can change through the generations."[52] Within the context of England, Scotland, Northern Ireland and Wales, the proper approach to 'nationality' is to categorise all of them as falling under the umbrella of British, and to regard the population as citizens of the United Kingdom.[53]

Colour

2.11 I shall not dwell on colour because it is self-explanatory. However, this is not without its difficulties, part of which I shall deal with under Chapters Seven and Eight when dealing with and discussing diversity awareness and inclusion, and training. It would not have escaped some people that the use of colour is more symbolic than a 'race.'

---

[50] Para. 29
[51] Equality Act 2010 Code of Practice, paras. 2.38 and 2.43
[52] Equality Act 2010 Code of Practice, paras. 2.45
[53] *Northern Joint Police Board (appellants) v Power (respondent)* [1997] IRLR 610

For example, being 'black.' Putting aside how one defines race, there is or could be a noun response to one's Nationality – I am British. The British are here. National Origin – I am of Grenadian national origin. I was born in Grenada. Ethnicity – I am Nigerian. I am black, an *adjective*, is a lot harder to frame in a similar racial framework. This has caused problems because it is the one area of identity that has evolved and not yet been settled. For example, ironically, even in the debates on the race relations Bills that we discussed earlier, people are referred to as 'coloured,' which would not be acceptable language to use today but would include people who are today defined as black. I shall deal with this later.

Caste

2.12   Finally, it is debateable whether 'caste' would fit under 'race,' 'religion or belief,' or both.

2.12.1 In *Chandhok and another v Tirkey (Equality and Human Rights Commission intervening)*,[54] the EAT held that, "That though "caste" as an autonomous concept did not presently come within s.9(1) many of the facts relevant in considering caste in many of its forms might be capable of doing so, since "ethnic origins" in s.9(1)(c) had a wide and flexible ambit, including characteristics determined by "descent.""

2.12.2 In the Explanatory Notes to the Act, 'the term "caste" denotes a hereditary, endogamous (marrying within the

---

[54] *[2015; IRLR 195; [2015] ICR 527; (2014) UKEAT/0190/14*

group) community associated with a traditional occupation and ranked accordingly on a perceived scale of ritual purity. It is generally (but not exclusively) associated with South Asia, particularly India, and its diaspora. It can encompass the four classes (varnas) of Hindu tradition (the Brahmin, Kshatriya, Vaishya and Shudra communities); the thousands of regional Hindu, Sikh, Christian, Muslim or other religious groups known as jatis; and groups amongst South Asian Muslims called biradaris. Some jatis regarded as below the varna hierarchy (once termed "untouchable") are known as Dalit.' A Minister is empowered by the Act to add 'caste' to the definition of race.[55]

Direct Discrimination

2.13 Under the Act, someone discriminates against another person if, because of a protected characteristic, being 'race' for our purposes, the former treats the latter less favourably than the former treats or would treat others. This amounts to *direct discrimination* and from this definition we can see that there are many strands. For sure, it is not simply that a claimant is of a different race to the alleged discriminator and, therefore, the alleged detrimental treatment about which the claimant complains is because of their race. Not only is there more needed to succeed in a claim, but a discriminator could, for example, discriminate against a person of the *same* race. Furthermore, the alleged treatment need not *necessarily* be because of the claimant's race or a

---

[55] s.9(5) Equality Act 2010

racial group of which they are a member. Let us break it down.

2.14 It is important to know the part or parts of 'race' on which one relies – for both a claimant and a respondent. For example, if colour is not the basis for the alleged discrimination but ethnicity *is*, it would be fruitless to argue that the comparator – the one to whom the less favourable treatment the claimant compares – is of a different colour, as this is not the reason for the alleged difference in treatment. Likewise, for the respondent. If the claimant alleges that they have been treated less favourably because of nationality of which there are currently, for example, six different types of British nationality – British citizenship; British overseas territories citizen; British overseas citizen; British subject; British national (overseas); and British protected person – it would be of little or no assistance to base their primary argument on the comparator's national origin if there is no overlap between the two – nationality and national origin.

...because of a protected characteristic...

2.15 "Simply to say that the conduct was unreasonable tells us nothing about the grounds for acting in that way. The fact that the victim is black [...] does no more than raise the possibility that the employer could have been influenced by unlawful discriminatory considerations. Absent some independent evidence supporting the conclusion that this was indeed the reason, no finding of discrimination can possibly be made."[56] It is important to note, for our purposes, "...*because of a protected characteristic*..." longhand does not mean, "...*because of the claimant's race*..." shorthand. The alleged treatment *may be* because of 'the' claimant's race but not *necessarily*. The claimant need only present a complaint because of 'a' race. In other words, the race in question does not have to be that of the claimant's race. For example, an English worker might be treated less favourably by her employer not because of her national origin but because her husband is Scottish. In this case, she is treated less favourably because of race, being Scottish, which is not a protected characteristic she *herself* possesses. This type of discrimination is frequently referred to as 'discrimination by association.'

2.16 Worthy of note is another form of discrimination against a complainant who does not possess the protected characteristic against which they were allegedly discriminated, and that is where the discriminator mistakenly believes the complainant to be of the race in question. For example, where the basis of the less favourable treatment of the Portuguese man is that the discriminator believed *mistakenly* that he was Spanish. This type of discrimination is frequently referred to as 'discrimination by perception.'

2.17 "All unlawful discriminatory treatment is unreasonable, but not all unreasonable treatment is discriminatory, and it is

---

[56] *The Law Society and others (appellants) v. Bahl (respondent) [2003] IRLR 640, para 94*

not shown to be so merely because the victim is…of a minority race or colour."[57] To establish unlawful discrimination, it is necessary to show that the employer's reason for acting was *because of* race. The race *must* be the cause of the treatment, otherwise it could not *reliably* be said that the treatment was *because* of race. However, race need not be the main or only cause for the treatment. Furthermore, the discriminator discriminates unlawfully even if they demonstrate that their motive was not to do so. Also, the discriminator is liable whether the discriminatory act is conscious or unconscious. As can be imagined, the latter is harder than the former to accept by the discriminator because, being unconscious, they are not conscious of their own actions – sometimes not even when subsequently pointed out! As Lord Prior of Brampton observed, during the "Race in the Workplace: The McGregor-Smith Review," on 24 April 2017, "Today, interview, selection and promotion processes in the workplace are the modern setting where intrinsic, subconscious bias now most evidently—but, as I have argued, by no means exclusively—plays out. We pick people "like us"; people who will "fit in"; people who will be part of our team: in other words, white, male and who want to play rugby at the weekends."[58]

…less favourable treatment…

---

[57] *The Law Society and others (appellants) v. Bahl (respondent) [2003] IRLR 640, para 94*
[58] House of Lords. Hansard HL, 24 April 2017, Vol. 782, col. 1256-1259

2.18 In its everyday use, *less favourable treatment* is a comparative term. But less *compared to* whom? The words 'treats' and 'would treat' serve similar purposes in that they refer to how the complainant is treated but the comparators are not the same. The word 'or' as in the part, "…the former *treats* the latter less favourably than the former treats or *would treat* others," is there to separate an *actual* comparator relied on i.e. X treats Y less favourably than X *treats* Others (A *named* person or persons). However, in some cases there may not be an actual person with whom X can compare themselves, which, but for the hypothetical comparator (would treat) would leave X's being unable to bring a claim for an alleged discrimination to which she or he has been subjected. Here, the law comes to the rescue because X could bring her/his claim by alleging that X treats Y less favourably than X *would treat* Others (A *hypothetical* person or persons).

2.19 Contrary to some beliefs, therefore, it is not enough for a complainant simply to state their 'race' and claim race discrimination without a comparator because they would fail to demonstrate *less favourable treatment* than either a *named* or *hypothetical* person or persons. The exception to needing a comparator is where the complainant is segregated from others if they are relying on race as being the reason for the alleged segregation.[59]

2.20 Crucially, a chosen comparator cannot be a randomly chosen person at the sole behest and discretion of the complainant. There must be some thought to ensure that

---

[59] s.13(5) of the Equality Act 2010

the chosen person is the *correct* comparator. So, whomever the complainant relies on as their comparator, there must be no material difference between the circumstances relating to each case.

2.21 It is important to note that there must be *less favourable* treatment not just a *difference* in treatment. The most common *less favourable* treatment relied upon is subjecting employees to detriments and dismissals. However, one does not have to be an employee to qualify to bring a claim. An *applicant* for a job is also entitled to bring a claim against a *prospective* employer. For example, a *prospective* employer would discriminate against an applicant by not offering them employment if the reason for doing so is because of race.[60]

Indirect Discrimination

2.22 If I had a penny for every time a person defined indirect discrimination as Person A discriminating against Person C via Person B (hence the 'indirect' notion), I would be a very wealthy man. Let me put this notion to rest because this is not what it is.

2.23 Firstly, let me briefly touch on and go back to direct discrimination. We have already discussed how Person A can discriminate against Person C unlawfully by treating the latter less favourably than, say, Person B. We can see how this would be 'direct' discrimination because the less

---

[60] See s.39(1) of the Equality Act 2010

favourable treated is directed towards and aimed at Person C. However, what would be the position if employer A applies a provision, criterion or practice (PCP), which, on the face of it, seems harmless and neutral but when implemented puts or would put, say, Person C and others sharing C's race at particular disadvantage when compared with those who do not share Person C's and others sharing C's race? In this case, we can see how there is a form of discrimination, only it is *not* directed towards and aimed at Person C, but Person C is nonetheless disadvantageously affected by the employer's application of the PCP.

PCPs

2.24 Regarding a *provision*, "If it is a requirement or condition then by virtue of Article 6 of the Burden of Proof Directive[61], it must also be a provision. It may not be a criterion or a practice, but it is quite plain that these three words or alternatives are not cumulative, and it is enough if it is a provision."[62] The most common provisions in employment are those that form part of a contract of employment and policies found in company and staff handbooks.

2.25 A *criterion* is a standard or principle by which judgments or decisions are made. The obvious criteria are those seen on application forms for a job where you see 'desired' and 'essentials'. Also, criteria are frequently set as the standards to be met for promotion.

---

[61] EC Burden of Proof Directive 97/80: Article 6
[62] *British Airways plc (appellants) v Starmer (respondent) [2005] IRLR 862*

2.26 A *practice* is the way things are done. It not necessarily written. For example, if everyone finished work at 6pm on Fridays that would be a practice if the contractual hours are to 5pm Monday to Friday. Here, of course, we have a provision that says the employee finishes at 5pm on Fridays but a practice of finishing at 6pm instead.

2.27 Therefore, PCPs can take many forms and, "should be construed widely so as to include, for example, any formal or informal policies, rules, practices, arrangements, criteria, conditions, prerequisites, qualifications or provisions. A provision, criterion or practice may also include decisions to do something in the future – such as a policy or criterion that has not yet been applied – as well as a 'one-off' or discretionary decision."[63] However, it is unlikely that a "one-off" decision would be held to be a PCP if it does not carry with it an indication that it will or would be done again in future if a hypothetical similar case arises. Therefore, there was held to be no PCP operated by a respondent because the alleged requirement was "a one-off act in the course of dealings with one individual."[64]

Indirect Discrimination compared with Direct Discrimination

2.28 Put simply, direct discrimination focuses primarily on equality of *treatment*. If Person A does not, as a matter of fact, 'treat' Person C less favourably than Person B (Person C's chosen comparator) then, obviously, the question of

---

[63] Equality Act 2010 Code of Practice, Para 4.5
[64] *Ishola v Transport for London* [2020] EWCA Civ 112

whether Person C was treated less favourably than Person B by Person A because of 'race' does not arise. Again, the emphasis is on *treatment* at this stage because the question of detriment does not arise if there is no preceding *less favourable treatment*. On the other hand, indirect discrimination examines whether the *effect, impact,* of implementing the PCP results in an unlevel playing field, which, therefore, puts or would put some at a particular disadvantage when compared with those who do not share their race.

2.29 Therefore, it is important to note that *direct* discrimination and *indirect* discrimination are mutually exclusive. Organisation A cannot be said to treat Person C less favourable than Person B and by the same act said to have indirectly discriminated against Person C (and potentially others), thus put Person C (and potentially others) at a particular disadvantage when compared to those not of Person C's (and potentially others') race, due to the application of the organisation's PCPs.

Justification

2.30 On reflection, one can see that some PCPs would be necessary for the running of the organisation in question and could be, therefore, objectively justified in that the organisation can show the PCPs to be proportionate means of achieving legitimate aims. In this case, the organisation would not be held liable for indirect discrimination. However, in the case of direction discrimination, there is no justification for an organisation/individual to treat another worker less favourably because of race. Therefore, if an organisation/individual were found to have done so, they would be liable for direct discrimination i.e. there is no defence of justification or that such treatment was a, "proportionate means of achieving legitimate aims."

2.31 In the following case, the appellant (and other appellants) was an immigration officer. The Home Office had a PCP that was a requirement to pass a Core Skills Assessment ('CSA') as a prerequisite to promotion to certain civil service grades. The CSA was a generic test required for each of those grades, irrespective of the particular role. All the appellants had, at some time, failed the CSA and were thus not, at that time, eligible for promotion. In fact, some of those who sat the test and failed had already been performing the roles on a temporary promotion basis, had excelled and, thus, were supported by their supervisors in their applications for the permanent roles. In 2010, a report commissioned by the Home Office revealed that Black and Minority Ethnic ('BME') candidates and older candidates had lower pass rates than white and younger candidates. No one knew why the proportion of BME or older candidates failing was significantly higher than the proportion of white or younger candidates failing. It was held that the appellants need not prove *why* the PCP relied upon put or would put them at a particular disadvantage.[65] Simply to prove that the PCP put or would put them at a particular disadvantage was

---

[65] *Essop and others v Home Office (UK Border Agency); Naeem v Secretary of State for Justice [2017] UKSC 27*

enough. Furthermore, an employer could still be liable even if the disadvantage suffered was found to be unconnected with the claimant's race. Again, all that was needed to be shown was that the racial group to which they belonged *existed* and that they had suffered a disadvantage.

Harassment

2.32　Being harassed with the act of harassment being unrelated to a protected characteristic – for our purposes, race – would not be a claim that the victim could bring under the Equality Act 2010. The act in question *must* be related to race. However, that is not all. There are other elements. The act must be unwanted by the alleged victim. This is the foundation. If one does not establish this, there would be no point in moving on to the other elements.

Unwanted by whom?

2.33　On the face of it, this seems obvious. To be clear, "The word 'unwanted' means essentially the same as 'unwelcome' or 'uninvited'. 'Unwanted' does not mean that express objection must be made to the conduct before it is deemed to be unwanted. A serious one-off incident can also amount to harassment."[66]

2.34　But what if two or more people witness the same act and some find it unwanted and some are fine with it i.e. the act is not unwanted? Does the latter override the former? In

---

[66] Equality Act 2010 Code of Practice, Para. 7.8

other words, does the mere fact that some do not find the act unwanted mean that the same act cannot or should not be deemed unwanted by others? Some would recognise this as banter versus harassment. One person's banter is another person's harassment. What is not unwanted – or actively wanted – by one person is unwanted by another. Clearly, it is down to the individual whether the act is wanted or unwanted. That means it would be no defence to a claim for an employer to say that it was or would be unreasonable for A to say that the banter on race was unwanted by her or him because B and C took no offence to the banter, and it was not unwanted by them. Once it has been established both that the conduct was unwanted and that it was related to race, we then turn our attention to the purpose or effect of the conduct.

The purpose or effect of the conduct

2.35 Before we look at what the purpose or effect of the conduct is supposed to have on the victim, it should be noted that the law requires the claimant to establish either the *purpose* or *effect* of the conduct, not both. Of course, both could be relevant, but only one is required to get over this hurdle. Also, the approach adopted for the two is different.

2.36 When examining the *purpose*, one need necessarily look at the motive of the alleged harasser, for it is only that person who can truly say what the purpose of their conduct was. Therein lies a potential problem because it is highly unlikely that one would admit that the purpose of their conduct was to harass the victim. Therefore, one would need to examine the motive of the harasser, which, naturally, has its obvious difficulties.

2.37 By comparison, the *effect* is easier because here the motive of the alleged harasser is irrelevant. Therefore, the source of banter would not be able to rely on a defence to a harassment claim that their purpose or intention was not to harass the victim but was just a bit of banter. So, when examining *effect* we must consider the *perception* of the victim, the other circumstances of the matter and whether it is reasonable for the conduct to have that effect. From these three elements we can see, for example, that there are both subjective (the perception of the victim) and objective (whether it is reasonable for the conduct to have that effect) parts when examining the effect of the unwanted conduct. Therefore, if I were to say that a colleague borrowed my eraser for two minutes longer than he had permission to and were to claim that this was harassment based on my race, that may well be my perception, but I think I might struggle to show that it was reasonable for that conduct to have that effect on me. However, 'the other circumstances of the matter' are also important and can cause problems or be of assistance.

Context

2.38 Here, we have a bank of judicial guidance commentary on which to rely for assistance. As stated by the Court of Appeal, "When assessing the effect of a remark, the context in which it is given is always highly material. Everyday experience tells us that a humorous remark between friends may have a very different effect than exactly the same words spoken vindictively by a hostile speaker. It is not importing intent into the concept of effect to say that intent will generally be relevant to assessing effect. It will also be relevant to deciding whether the response of the alleged victim is reasonable."[67]

2.39 It was reiterated by the EAT that, "context is everything," and that, "it may be a mistake to focus upon a remark in isolation. A tribunal is entitled to take the view, as we see it, that a remark, however unpleasant and however unacceptable, is a remark made in a particular context; it is not simply a remark standing on its own [...] Words that are hostile may contain a reference to a particular characteristic of the person to whom and against whom they are spoken. Generally, a tribunal might conclude that in consequence the words themselves are that upon which there must be focus and that they are discriminatory, but a tribunal, in our view, is not obliged to do so. The words are to be seen in context;"[68]

2.40 For the purposes of this section, I respectfully adapt and adopt an example given by the EAT to emphasise the point. "We think a simple illustration will suffice to show why this must be the law."[69] Suppose that Y, an Antiguan man,

---

[67] *Grant (appellant) v. HM Land Registry (respondent) and Equality and Human Rights Commission (interverner) - [2011] IRLR 748, para. 13*
[68] *Warby v Wunda Group plc UKEAT/0434/11/CEA (Transcript)*
[69] *Nazir and another v Asim - [2010] ICR 1225, para. 71*

shouts and swears loudly at Z, a Vincentian woman. He does so immediately after Z accidentally spills a cup of coffee over his clothing; and prior to this Y had never shouted or sworn at Z. It would be absurd to ignore the spilling of the cup of coffee on Y when deciding if there is a prima facie case that he harassed Z related to race. The spilling of the coffee is not merely an explanation; it is also part of the context in which the tribunal must decide whether there is a prima facie case of racial harassment. And in the case whether Y's conduct is thought to be reasonable.

2.41 Take, for example, a situation where a level of banter has been acceptable at work between a group of workers, which includes the claimant. At some point the claimant decides either that the banter is no longer wanted and it becomes *unwanted* conduct or is of the view that the banter has gone over and above a level than what *was* acceptable and is now *unwanted*. In this case, the claimant would have to make their position clear that the conduct in question is unwanted, otherwise they run the risk and danger of giving the impression that the conduct is either not unwanted or it is wanted as was the position *before*. There could, of course, be a difficulty for employers because unless they can demonstrate that they took all reasonable steps to prevent the conduct in question they will be liable for the harassment by their employees. I shall deal with liability later. However, in the meantime, training is paramount to educate employees that there is a level of banter that is unacceptable in the workplace and that *no* banter should relate to a colleague's race – a zero tolerance environment.

In that case, the risk of a successful harassment case is substantially reduced if not eliminated.

2.42 However, if an unwanted conduct is deemed to be related to the victim's race, that conduct must have the purpose or effect of either violating the victim's dignity or creating an intimidating, hostile, degrading, humiliating or offensive environment for the victim. In short, therefore, a victim would succeed in a claim of harassment on the verb/noun pairing of *either* the said 'violating/dignity' or 'creating/environment.' Again, the victim does not need to prove both – i.e. the violation of the dignity *and* the creation of the environment. Either will suffice.

Harassment and Direct Discrimination[70]

2.43 Finally, whereas it is not inconceivable that someone could argue successfully that they had not treated another less favourably than a named or hypothetical comparator because they *treat everyone the same* (thus no less favourable treatment), the same conduct related to race may *still* be unwanted and which violates the victim's dignity or creates an intimidating, hostile, degrading, humiliating or offensive environment for the victim. In consequence, the same conduct may not amount to direct discrimination because of race but may amount to harassment because it relates to race etc.

---

[70] https://youtu.be/hV7nPCnPc1I

Victimisation

2.44   Like harassment, victimisation has a specific meaning under the Equality Act 2010.[71] It is not victimisation as used in common parlance i.e. simply to target someone for harm of some kind. Under the 2010 Act, a person is victimised if they have been treated detrimentally because they have done a protected act or the victimiser believes that the victim has done, or may do, a protected act. Let us break it down.

Protected act

2.45   Effectively, a person is protected from being harmed because, in good faith, they are bringing proceedings under the 2010 Act; giving evidence or information in connection with proceedings under the 2010 Act; doing any other thing for the purposes of or in connection with the 2010 Act; and or making an allegation (whether or not express) that they or another person has contravened the 2010 Act. The list is comprehensive and wide.

2.46   Therefore, if someone (claimant) takes their employer to the employment tribunal, alleging race discrimination and the employer takes issue with this allegation, which results in the employer refusing to give the claimant a pay rise because they brought a claim against them, this would amount to victimisation of the claimant. The same would apply where an employee raises, for example, a grievance alleging harassment related to race and the employer or colleagues

---

[71] See https://youtu.be/PVJQUBQwdUY

subject the employee to a detriment because of the harassment content of the grievance. To be clear, the protection is not only for those who raise complaints or issue a claim, but also extends to anyone who supports them. For example, an employee who accompanies the aggrieved employee, raising the complaint of racial harassment or the employee who provides evidence at an employment tribunal hearing in support of a claimant alleging, for example, indirect race discrimination would also be protected from being subjected to any detriment because of their involvement.

2.47 The complainant does not have to use words such as 'discrimination,' 'harassment,' or, for that matter, 'victimisation' for there to be a protected act. As made clear by the EAT, "There is no need for the allegation to refer to the legislation, or to allege a contravention, but the gravamen of the allegation must be such that, if the allegation were proved, the alleged act would be a contravention of the legislation."[72] If a woman says to her employer, 'I am aggrieved with you for holding back my research and career development' her statement is not protected. If a woman says to her employer, 'I am aggrieved with you for holding back my research and career development because I am Indian' or 'because you are favouring the Scottish workers in the department over the Welsh,' her statement would be protected even if there was no reference to the Equality Act 2010 or to a contravention of it.

---

[72] *Beneviste v Kingston University [2006] UKEAT/0393/05, para. 29*

2.48 The protection is not only afforded to those who prove that the employer has contravened the 2010 Act in some way, it is also for those who *believe* that the employer has contravened it but was mistaken. In other words, someone raises a grievance in *good faith* alleging that they have been treated less favourably than a colleague because of race. But the grievance was not upheld, which the aggrieved accepts as a fair outcome, because the treatment that was the subject of the grievance was for a reason unrelated to race. The employer cannot punish the employee for having made 'false' allegations against the employer and or colleague.

Direct Discrimination and Victimisation

2.49 It is not uncommon for a complainant to raise a complaint of direct discrimination and victimisation. For example, an employee raises a grievance against her manager, alleging less favourable treatment because of the race of her partner. The grievance is not upheld and subsequently her manager refuses to engage with her at work whilst engaging with other colleagues of all races, including those who belong to the complainant's racial group. When asked why she refuses to engage with the complainant the manager states openly that it is because of the grievance against her, "calling me a racist." Here, we can see how the manager and employer may have a defence to an allegation of direct discrimination and fail on the victimisation because the reason given for the manager's treatment of the complainant is that the latter made a protected act, in that she made, "an allegation (whether or not express) that [the manager] has contravened the 2010 Act," being, "discriminated against her because of race." The above is not uncommon. Therefore, it is easy to see how an accused could be found not to have unlawfully discriminated against another because of race but victimised them because of their being aggrieved for their having been accused of discrimination in the first place.

2.50   Of course, an act may also *not* be victimisation, even if the complainant made a protected act, but may be direct discrimination. Staying with the above scenario. Say, for example, the complainant above raises a further grievance against the manager that her manager refuses to engage with her at work whilst engaging with other colleagues but she does not allege that the reason for doing so is that she complained before, which, as we have established was a protected act. To ensure impartiality, the employer engages services of an external person who has no knowledge of the first grievance/protected act and does not uphold the latest grievance. The complainant is of the view that her grievance was not upheld because of race, which may or may not be meritorious. However, were she to bring a claim of victimisation she would fail because the decision maker could not have victimised her without having knowledge of the protected act, being the first grievance. In other words, the decision maker cannot be influenced by a protected act of which she has no knowledge to be able to victimise the aggrieved.

Racism and Race Discrimination

2.51   Let us remind ourselves of some key words. Regarding direct discrimination, we see that the discriminator *treats* the victim less favourably than the discriminator *treats* or would *treat* others. Regarding indirect discrimination, we see that the discriminator *applies* to the victim a PCP that is discriminatory in relation to the victim's race. Regarding Harassment, we see that the discriminator *engages* in unwanted conduct related to the victim's race. Regarding Victimisation, we see that the discriminator victimises the victim if the discriminator *subjects* the victim to a detriment because the victim does a protected act or the discriminator believes that the victim has done, or may do, a protected act. What emerges from these are that the verbs to apply, to engage and to subject are not dependent on discriminators' ideologies. In other words, the law is seeking to protect the victim from treatment, not seeking to change or punish the ideologies to which a discriminator may or may not subscribe. It is important that a claimant and, for that matter, a respondent bear this distinction in mind.

Institutional Racism

2.52 The Macpherson report examined extensively the various definitions of 'institutional racism' and concluded at 6.34 the following:

> Taking all that we have heard and read into account we grapple with the problem. For the purposes of our Inquiry the concept of institutional racism which we apply consists of:
> **The collective failure of an organisation to provide an appropriate and professional service to people**

because of their colour, culture, or ethnic origin. It can be seen or detected in processes, attitudes and behaviour which amount to discrimination through unwitting prejudice, ignorance, thoughtlessness and racist stereotyping which disadvantage minority ethnic people.

It persists because of the failure of the organisation openly and adequately to recognise and address its existence and causes by policy, example and leadership. Without recognition and action to eliminate such racism it can prevail as part of the ethos or culture of the organisation. It is a corrosive disease.[73]

2.53 'Institutional Racism' is discussed in Chapter 8.

---

[73] https://assets.publishing.service.gov.uk/government/uploads/system/uploads/attachment_data/file/277111/4262.pdf

~ CHAPTER THREE ~

"There is discrimination and bias at every stage of an individual's career, and even before it begins."

Baroness McGregor-Smith CBE [74]

---

[74] The McGregor-Smith Review, Race in the workplace, "THE TIME FOR TAKING IS OVER. NOW IS THE TIME TO ACT," February 2017, Forward, p.3

GRIEVANCE & DISCIPLINARY

3.1 This chapter deals with what happens if a worker believes they have been discriminated against, harassed and or victimised. It also deals with employers' responsibilities when dealing with grievances in the event that an employee raises a grievance. Finally, I deal with disciplinary matters, which may or may not be linked to the grievance. For example, if a grievance is upheld where the aggrieved alleges discrimination, harassment and or victimisation, should the culprit face disciplinary measures?

Grievance

3.2 In order to deal with grievances, we first need to understand what a grievance is.

What is a Grievance?

3.3 There is no one fixed definition of what a grievance is. However, put succinctly, a grievance is a problem or complaint raised by an employee to their employer and the way in which that grievance (the *problem* or *complaint* raised) is handled is prescribed by the employer's grievance procedure.

3.4 The ACAS[75] Guide *Discipline and Grievances at Work* (2020) (the Guide)[76], which complements the ACAS Code of

---

[75] Advisory, Conciliation and Arbitration Service
[76] https://www.acas.org.uk/acas-guide-to-discipline-and-grievances-at-

Practice on Disciplinary and Grievance Procedures Code of Practice 1 (2015) (the Code)[77], defines a grievance as, 'a problem or concern that an employee has about their work, working conditions or relationships with colleagues or managers.'[78] It also gives a non-exhaustive list of issues that may cause grievances, which includes, amongst other things, terms and conditions of employment; work relations; bullying and harassment; working environment; and discrimination. Regarding grievances about fellow employees, the Guide says, 'Employees may complain that they have been bullied, harassed or discriminated against by another employee or may complain about another employee's attitude.' Therefore, the nature or content of a grievance is very wide but primarily personal to the aggrieved employee and the effect the subject of the grievance has on them together with the preferred remedy sought by the employee.

ACAS Code

3.5 Principally, parties to a contract can agree whatever they so wish provided it is not unlawful or illegal. So, what about a company's grievance procedure? For ease of reference, I am referring to a *written* procedure. Having a procedure that falls below an acceptable (minimum) standard could still land the employer in trouble even if the parties expressly agreed to it and it was followed strictly without any material

---

work
[77] https://www.acas.org.uk/acas-code-of-practice-for-disciplinary-and-grievance-procedures/html#the-code-of-practice
[78] Page 77

deviation. For example, it would be unlawful, and therefore the term ineffective, to prevent an employee from being accompanied at their grievance hearing or to prevent them from having a right of appeal.

3.6 At this point we introduce properly a very important document with which managers, HR practitioners and supervisors alike ought to familiarise themselves. The Code is a statutory code and provides, 'basic practical guidance' to employers and employees and sets out principles for handling grievance situations in the workplace. It sets out the minimum standards to be met. Therefore, a company is at liberty to use the Code on which to build their own procedure. For example, some may add protective provisions if a grievance raises issues of *harassment & bullying*. Some may allow for a different policy to be invoked if the employee raises an allegation of *discrimination* against a colleague, and, as a way of complying with a 'zero tolerance' policy in the workplace, offer a 'guarantee' (within reason) that in the event of the grievance being upheld the discriminator is *automatically* subjected to disciplinary measures. In fact, in some cases a *hybrid* grievance procedure applies where the grievance raises such issues (discrimination, harassment, bullying etc.). A failure on the part of any person to observe any provision of the Code will not in *itself* render them liable to any proceedings.

A right to have the grievance heard

3.7 The relationship between employee and employer is governed by the terms of their agreement, which is in the form of a contract. However, not all terms of a contract need necessarily be expressed (orally or in writing) in order for them to be effective. For example, it is an implied term in a contract of employment that employers will reasonably and promptly afford a reasonable opportunity to their employees to obtain redress of any grievance they may have.[79] In *Goold*,[80] the Employment Appeal Tribunal (EAT) held that, 'the right to obtain redress against a grievance is fundamental for very obvious reasons. The working environment may well lead to employees experiencing difficulties, whether because of the physical conditions under which they are required to work, or because of a breakdown in human relationships, which can readily occur when people of different backgrounds and sensitivities are required to work together, often under pressure.' Therefore, every employee has the right to have their grievance heard whether or not they have an express provision within their contract of employment.

Impartiality

3.8 Regarding the same person hearing both the grievance and the purported appeal, the EAT said, 'The right to an appeal

---

[79] *WA Goold (Pearmark) Ltd (appellants) v. McConnell and another (respondents) [1995] IRLR 516*
[80] *WA Goold (Pearmark) Ltd (appellants) v. McConnell and another (respondents) [1995] IRLR 516*, para. 12

in respect of a grievance is important both as a feature of the [employer]'s own grievance procedure and of the [then Code]. It is a significant right in the employment context. It is not easy to see why an organisation the size of the [employer] should have been unable to make provision for an impartial hearing by a manager not previously involved.'[81] A grievance or disciplinary appeal, 'should be dealt with impartially and, wherever possible, by a manager who has not previously been involved in the case.'[82] In consequence, to avoid any potential allegations of bias or partiality it is strongly advised that employers seek to have a person conduct an appeal who has had no previous involvement in the subject matter of the grievance.

Contractual and Non-Contractual Procedure

3.9   Some contracts will express the procedure to be adopted and, usually contained within the company (or staff) handbook, the process to be followed, and state whether the procedure and process are contractual or non-contractual. This, however, is not to be confused with the implied term of employees' rights to have their grievances heard, the *objective* of the employer is to act reasonably and promptly in affording the employee the reasonable opportunity to obtain the said redress about which we discussed earlier. This is about prescribing a contractual procedure (*how* the grievance will be undertaken – investigation by an independent external

---

[81] *Blackburn v Aldi Stores [2013] IRLR 846*
[82] The Code, paras 27 and 43

person/investigator interviewing the aggrieved employee first) or process (*what* is being undertaken – an investigation etc), but rather to do with

3.10 In *Taylor v Secretary of State for Scotland* [83] doubt was raised initially over whether a new equal opportunities policy contained in a circular, effectively announcing that no one in the service should be discriminated against on stipulated grounds, and applying it, 'to everything we do,' formed part of a contract of employment. It was found that the policy *did* form part of the contract, as the practice in the prison service was for changes and additions to prison officers' contracts, following negotiations between the employer and the unions, to be notified to them by means of circulars such as that by which the equal opportunities policy was circulated. Also, if new policies or their changes are introduced to the employee in the same way as, for example, proposed variations to a contract and are therefore accepted by the employee in the same or similar way then there is a good argument for suggesting that the parties are treating it as contractual as opposed to *simply* good practice. But, naturally, such a case would turn on its own facts. For example, in *Grant v South-West Trains Ltd*[84] the court held that the employer's equal opportunities policy, which provided that no one was to receive less favourable treatment on grounds of sexual preference, was not incorporated into the employee's contract of employment. It was a statement of policy in general, idealistic terms, and

---

[83] *(HL) [2000] ICR 595*
[84] *[1998] IRLR 188*

not of contractual obligations. There was no evidence of any contractual intention on the part of the employer or employee. No obligations are put upon the employer by the policy, and the obligation on the employee to act "in the spirit of the policy" was of the vaguest kind.

Written Grievance Procedure

3.11　Here, we are concerned with the benefits of the employer having a written procedure. As stated in the Code, 'Fairness and transparency are promoted by developing and using rules and procedures for handling disciplinary and grievance situations. These should be set down in writing, be specific and clear.'[85] There are obvious benefits to having the grievance procedure in writing for both the employer and the employee. It informs the parties with certainty the procedure to follow. An *ad hoc* arrangement would lack transparency, could lead to chaos and likely to lead to gross inconsistencies as one manager adopts a procedure that is materially different to another manager within the same organisation, dealing with a grievance of similar facts in similar circumstances. Clearly, this would not be ideal and potentially harmful to employee/employer relations, especially as the Code states that, 'Employers and employees should act consistently.'[86]

---

[85] Para. 2
[86] Para. 4

No written procedure

3.12   In *Goold*, the employer had no grievance procedure – written or otherwise – in place, as the, 'chairman said he was well-known to see any employee who has a grievance or other problem.' Two employees had raised grievances over the effects on their income, following a company reorganisation. Their manager said he would address it but failed to do so satisfactorily. In consequence, the employees sought to see the chairman but were told by his secretary that they had to go through the same manager with whom they were dissatisfied. The next day they resigned, claiming constructive dismissal. They subsequently presented a complaint to the employment tribunal, which decided in their favour. The tribunal considered whether the employer was in such serious breach of its obligations under the contracts of employment as to entitle the employees to leave as they did and claim constructive dismissal. Not only did the employer not have a written grievance procedure but the tribunal noted that neither of the employees had been given a written statement of particulars of employment[87] that would have specified the person to whom they could apply for the purpose of seeking redress of their grievances and the procedure. The tribunal was of the view

---

[87] As of 6 April 2020, among other things, s.1 of the Employment Rights Act 1996 states, "Where a worker begins employment with an employer, the employer shall give to the worker a written statement of particulars of employment…[T]he statement must be given not later than the beginning of the employment."

that any grievance procedure should have incorporated within it some kind of time limit, 'so as to ensure that grievances were nipped in the bud' and a failure to do so amounted to a breach of contract, entitling the employees to resign in consequence. The employer appealed unsuccessfully to the EAT who said, amongst other things, 'It is clear therefore, that Parliament considered that good industrial relations requires employers to provide their employees with a method of dealing with grievances in a proper and timeous fashion. This is also consistent, of course, with the [then Code].' The Code states that, 'Employers and employees should raise and deal with issues promptly and should not unreasonably delay meetings, decisions or confirmation of those decisions.'[88]

3.13 As *Goold* demonstrates it is not just an outcome of a grievance that could lead an employee to claim that as a result they deemed themselves constructively dismissed but, also, the procedure adopted (if at all!). Therefore, it is of equal importance that grievances are dealt with both within some kind of reasonable time limit/frame and dealt with promptly.

Written Statement of Particulars of Employment

3.14 The written statement of particulars of employment is frequently confused to be the contract of employment. The two are not the same. Where an employee begins employment with an employer, the employer shall give to

---

[88] Para. 4

the employee a written statement of particulars of employment not later than the beginning of the employment.[89] An employee should have both a contract and the statutory required Written Statement of Particulars. A contract of employment contains the agreed terms (express or implied) that govern the relationship between the employer and the employee. Whereas, the written statement of particulars states the main terms that legislation dictates must be provided by the employer to the employee to fulfil its statutory obligations.

3.15 Whether or not the grievance procedure is contractual, the statement of particulars of employment must *still* include a note specifying (by description or otherwise) a person to whom the employee can apply for the purpose of seeking redress of any grievance relating to their employment, the manner in which any such application should be made, and where there are further steps consequent on any such application, explaining those steps or referring to the provisions of a document ensuring that it is reasonably accessible to the employee.[90]

The Grievance

3.16 If an employee has a grievance, they should make it absolutely clear what their complaint is and whether they wish their complaint to be dealt with informally or formally. Many written grievance policies will state that if the

---

[89] s.1 of Employment Rights Act 1996
[90] s.3(1)(b)(ii), s.3(1)(c) Employment Rights Act 1996

employee has a grievance then, ideally, it should be dealt with informally – at the employee's election – and if not dealt with to the employee's satisfaction they may wish to raise it formally. However, when dealing with allegations as serious as discrimination because of race, harassment related to race and victimisation, I am of the view that these are allegations of so serious a nature that they should be raised and dealt with formally. I feel that to raise it informally, especially where an employer expresses that it has a zero tolerance on such matters, leaves room for diluting the importance of the complaint.

3.17 Furthermore, when raised informally, which will entail nothing more than a chat to an appropriate person (normally a supervisor or manager), there is no *real* outcome. The culprit, presumably, will be spoken to and no more. However, what happens if the culprit were to accept/admit the charge? As the grievance was raised informally, there might be a reluctance on the part of the employer to take the matter, which might otherwise have been deemed *very* serious had it been raised formally, any further, if any only to suggest that the culprit attends an appropriate course or undertakes appropriate training. Also, of course, if such a complaint is dealt with informally, whereas the culprit might be facing disciplinary measures for the accepted/admitted acts in question, that is highly unlikely to happen in this case. Notwithstanding all this, however, there are a multitude of reasons why an employee may wish to address their concerns informally and that would be their sole choice.

3.18 For example, during a conversation with an HR director of a multinational company, he raised the following with me. A manager of the company had received an informal complaint that a member of staff had overheard a colleague referring to people as 'coloured' and took offence to this term being used 'today'. He wondered whether the use of that language breached one of their policies, which would lead to disciplinary measures or was this a matter that could be dealt with informally with training. He confessed to being torn as to *right* approach to take. The manager spoke to the colleague who said that she simply wanted the culprit spoken to about the use of such archaic language in the workplace, which the manager did. However, after speaking to the culprit the company commissioned further training addressing issues raised and lessons learnt from the complaint. No disciplinary measures were deemed necessary.

3.19 Therefore, it is and would be better to raise one's concerns informally than *not* to raise their concerns at all. Otherwise, if such is not even brought to the attention of the employer at all, the employer may not be able to address the matter – as it may be unaware of the behaviour, especially if the acts complained of are done 'innocently' or covertly – or, worse, the acts continue to the detriment of the victim's wellbeing.

Formal Grievance Process and Procedure

3.20 Having set out clearly what the grievance is in writing and sent it to the appropriate person in accordance with the

Grievance Procedure, the employee should be invited to a meeting by the employer to discuss their grievance without delay, which the employee and their companion should make an effort to attend. The employee has a right to be accompanied at the meeting by a fellow worker, a trade union representative, or an official employed by a trade union. The companion is allowed to participate in the hearing, "to put and sum up the worker's case, respond on behalf of the worker to any views expressed at the meeting and confer with the worker during the hearing," but does not have, "the right to answer questions on the worker's behalf, address the hearing if the worker does not wish it or prevent the employer from explaining their case."[91]

3.21 The person Chairing the meeting should, ideally, be someone who has been trained in anti-discriminatory practices and attended equal opportunities courses. These, I believe, would make the Chair attuned to the nuances of some complaints that may not appear on the surface to an untrained person to be a problem. For example, when hearing a complaint of harassment related to race when, on the face of it to an untrained eye, it may appear to be nothing more than a little harmless banter. It is important that the person hearing the grievance has a thorough understanding of the nature of the grievance and why the aggrieved feels the way they do. The Chair should also ascertain what the aggrieved is seeking as a resolution. The Chair should approach the grievance with an open mind and avoid forming a view *before* hearing the grievance and all

---

[91] Para. 37 of the Code

the necessary investigations have been undertaken. It is important that the Chair holds a meeting with the subject of the grievance to hear their side and response to the grievance. It may be necessary to interview other people who may be able to assist with the investigation, especially when there are disputes of fact. Forming a view based on conflicting evidence can be a difficult task. However, serious thought has to be given to weigh up the evidence and form a view based on why one set of evidence is more likely to be true than another.

3.22 Allegations of race discrimination, harassment related to race and victimisation are very serious and can, therefore, be stressful both for the aggrieved and the accused, which the employer should bear in mind when dealing with the grievance and the related investigations. I should state, however, the person hearing the grievance is to investigate the grievance and reach a conclusion on what has been found rather than be swayed by the consequence of upholding or not upholding the grievance. For example, where there is conflicting evidence where the Chair is minded to believe, for example, the aggrieved over the accused, it would wrong for the Chair to be influenced *not* to uphold that part of the grievance because, to do so, would land the accused into trouble! Likewise, it would be wrong for the Chair to be persuaded by the accused but find in favour of the aggrieved simply to appease that person. Once a decision has been reached then that decision should be communicated to the aggrieved in writing, setting out clearly what that decision is, the reasons for that decision, any action to be taken to resolve the matter and the employee's right of appeal. If the employee exercises a right of appeal, they are allowed to be accompanied again with the same rights. Many appeals are not a rehearing of the grievance. The appeal procedure and process should make it clear if it is a rehearing or not. So, if the right of appeal is limited to where the employee believes that the decision was wrong and is to give reasons, there is little to no value in the appeal simply repeating the nature of the grievance. The employee must state why they *believe* the grievance *outcome* was wrong. For example, the Chair omitted to interview the only independent witness to the conduct in question and had the Chair interviewed that person it is highly likely that the Chair would have reached a different (presumably, favourable) conclusion. The appeal decision is final. If the employee is unhappy with the appeal decision they can present their complaint to the Employment Tribunal, which I shall deal with in the next Chapter. Below is an example of how a letter raising a formal grievance may look.

3.23   *Letter 1*

Dear Sarah,

<u>Formal Grievance</u>

Please accept this letter as a formal grievance in accordance with the grievance policy.

On Friday, I was sat on the same table as Phil who repeatedly made racist comments such as, "XXX,"

"YYY," and "ZZZ." I told him to stop his conduct, but he told me that he was not talking about me or my 'kind' and that I should not have an issue and continued. I was appalled by his conduct, found his comments to be deeply offensive and felt harassed by his inappropriate conduct about race. I did not want this conduct around me and made it absolutely clear to Phil, but he continued nevertheless.

On Monday I spoke to Sylvia about his behaviour, but, sadly, she seemed to condone his conduct by saying that he probably had too much to drink and that I should, "loosen up a little."

I am disappointed that despite our policies on equality and anti-discrimination, the company seems to condone Phil's racist behaviour.

3.24 Although I have used the words, "Formal Grievance," as the heading, an aggrieved does not need to label it as such or, for that matter, need to even use the word 'grievance'.

3.25 The nature of some grievances, regarding allegations such as race discrimination, harassment and victimisation, are sometimes dealt with under a policy that, in the event that the grievance is upheld, *necessarily* invokes the disciplinary procedure.

3.26   *Letter 2*

Dear Phil,

<u>Invitation to Disciplinary Hearing</u>

Further to Rachel's grievance against you, regarding your conduct at the company function on 13 December, in which she made clear to you that your comments such as, "XXX," "YYY," and "ZZZ," were unwanted by her and which were clearly related to race, I now invite you to attend a disciplinary meeting in accordance with the Equality, Diversity and Inclusion Policy. As you know from your induction training and other courses you have attended, we take allegations of harassment very seriously. We are an equal opportunities employer and have a zero tolerance on unlawful discrimination, harassment and victimisation. As you know, the grievance was upheld and, therefore, I believe you have a case to answer to the allegation that on 13 December 2019 you engaged in a conduct that was unwanted by Rachel and that she told you to stop but you nevertheless continued. Your conduct was related to race and had the purpose or effect of creating an offensive environment for her.

I enclose a copy of the Equality, Diversity and Inclusion and Disciplinary policies for your information. You will note that examples of offences normally regarded as gross misconduct include, amongst other things, "unlawful discrimination or harassment." Therefore, a possible sanction for your conduct could be summary dismissal.

You have the right to be accompanied by a fellow worker, a trade union representative, or an official employed by a trade union…

Disciplinary Procedure and Process

What is a Disciplinary?

3.27 Primarily, a disciplinary is part of a company's internal process for dealing with matters that relate to its employees' *conduct* and *capability*. Whereas grievances are raised *by the employee*, the employee is subjected to disciplinary *by the employer*. As expected, conduct or misconduct can take many forms. The relevant legislation, the Employment Rights Act 1996, does not use language such as *mis*conduct or *gross mis*conduct, therefore there is no statutory definition of 'conduct.'[92]

3.28 However, 'Disciplinary rules should give examples of acts which the employer regards as acts of gross misconduct.'[93] Hence, in a company or staff handbook there is usually a non-exhaustive list of what may amount to gross

---

[92] s98(2)(b) of the Employment Rights Act 1996
[93] The Code, para. 24

misconduct, where summary dismissal may be deemed the appropriate sanction. The Guide gives some examples of offences that are normally regarded as gross misconduct, which includes, amongst others, unlawful discrimination or harassment. It is important to note that an employee found to be guilty of an act of gross misconduct is *not* automatically dismissed, but they *may be* summarily dismissed. In other words, it ought to be discretionary, taking into account any mitigation, on the appropriate sanction.

3.29 The same level of fairness afforded to a worker raising a grievance is given to a person facing disciplinary. However, let us start at the beginning of the process.

Investigation

3.30 It can be somewhat confusing to an employee who is facing disciplinary measures when it comes to an investigation into a disciplinary matter. Under many company policies, an employee can be disciplined for unlawfully discriminating against an employee or harassing them. The first step to take would be to investigate the matter to ascertain the facts. Although the nature of the investigation is often detailed in the disciplinary procedure, the investigation is a 'fact finding' exercise only. Therefore, at the investigatory stage the employee under the investigation is neither deemed guilty of the charge nor being disciplined. Furthermore, as this is a fact finding exercise the employee is not entitled to be accompanied at an investigatory meeting unless allowed under the company's disciplinary policy, which is very rare. Sometimes an employee may be suspended whilst the company undertakes and completes the investigation. Again, although this forms part of the disciplinary procedure it is not a sign of guilt on the part of the subject of the investigation. If suspended, this should be kept to a minimum and, as the employee is deemed innocent during this period, the employee should be entitled to their full pay. If the investigator concludes that the employee is guilty of any of the charges, it would be recommended that the employee should face disciplinary measures because they have a case to answer.

Disciplinary Procedure

3.31 The employee should be told in writing that they have a case to answer on the charges investigated, the reasons for reaching this view and the evidence relied upon. The employee would be invited to a disciplinary meeting without delay, giving them sufficient time to prepare and the right to be accompanied. The person chosen to Chair the disciplinary hearing should be a suitable impartial person – in both the sense of fairness and one who has had no previous involvement in the matter – who ideally had attended anti-discriminatory, equal opportunity courses etc. The invitation to the disciplinary meeting should also state the range of possible sanctions. For example, if the most severe outcome could be summary dismissal for the said race discrimination or harassment then the employee should be informed of this in writing. The employee ought to be given every right to answer the charges. The hearing should be adjourned if the Chair believes that they need to undertake further investigations. At the conclusion of the disciplinary meeting the Chair should take their time to consider all that has been discussed and to weigh up all the evidence before making a finding. Also, the Chair should consider any mitigating factors. For example, in the case of harassment related to race, which the accused said resulted from previously accepted 'banter' around the workplace, the employer may find that this is a wider concern to be addressed and, although culpable, the ultimate sanction of dismissal in the circumstances might not be fair for what is in essence a company cultural issue of which the culprit just happens to be a part. Of course, the employee would still be guilty of the charge but, as discussed in Chapter Two, "the other circumstances of the case," are also relevant.

3.32   If an employee raised a grievance of race discrimination, harassment related to race or victimisation against a colleague, which was upheld, it might be difficult for the accused to avoid a sanction under the disciplinary procedure, especially when the employer has subscribed to a 'zero tolerance' on such behaviour/conduct. It might be bewildering to understand how an accused avoids a sanction in the circumstances. For example, a grievance was upheld under a grievance policy, the result of which was that the aggrieved has been found to be unlawfully discriminated against, racially harassed or victimised, but no disciplinary action took place under the same company's disciplinary policy would probably leave the aggrieved puzzled. Puzzling as it may appear, however, a remedy demanded by an aggrieved under a grievance policy cannot be that the culprit be disciplined. That choice would remain solely with the employer.

3.33 The disciplinary outcome should be in writing, giving reasons for the conclusion. The conclusion and reasons must be clear. If the employee is to be sanctioned – normally an oral warning, first written warning, final written warning or dismissal – they need to be told clearly why this is the case with reference to the disciplinary policy. Whatever the sanction, the employee ought to be given a right of appeal. Some policies make it clear that it does not have to follow the disciplinary procedure if the employee has less than two years' continuous service, which is in relation to cases concerning unfair dismissal. However, here we are discussing a sanction that arose from an employee being found to be guilty of race discrimination or harassment, which was governed either by the disciplinary policy or another company policy (Discrimination, Harassment, Equal Opportunities, Diversity & Awareness etc.) dealing specifically with such complaints. As with a grievance, the employee has the right to be accompanied and the decision on an appeal is final.

Conduct done in the course of employment

3.34 Sometimes it is difficult to distinguish between an employee's conduct done in the course of their employment and one that is not. For example, if an employee racially harasses a colleague at the company's party held after working hours, would the company be liable? If yes, what is the position if the harassment takes place at the 'after party' with a group colleagues? The answers will turn on the facts of the case. In a case involving the conduct of an employee on social media, an employer was held not liable for its employee's posting of a racially offensive image on Facebook. It was held that, "The tribunal was entitled to find that the posting was not done in the course of employment." As observed by the EAT in the same case, "Furthermore, the employer may, depending on its policy, be entitled to take disciplinary action in respect of a Facebook post which it considered to be potentially damaging of its reputation. However, the fact that the employer considers it appropriate to take such action does not mean that the conduct in question is necessarily done in the course of employment. The employer can, for example, take action, again depending on policies, against an employee where it transpires that he or she has committed criminal acts outside employment, or acts which are otherwise considered offensive or unacceptable. An employee found to be chanting racist slogans at a football match, for example, might be regarded by an employer as engaging in conduct worthy of censure. However, no reasonable person would regard such conduct as being done in the course of employment, unless there was shown to be some connection between attendance at the football match and employment that suggested otherwise."[94]

---

[94] *Forbes (appellant) v LHR Airport Ltd (respondent) [2019] IRLR 890 at 895*

~ CHAPTER FOUR ~

"[T]he question we must consider when we are thinking about the racial discrimination which undoubtedly exists at present is whether the climate can be altered in some degree by legislation"

Sir Dingle Foot[95]

---

[95] 23 April 1968, House of Commons

EMPLOYMENT TRIBUNAL I

4.1 If a worker believes they have been unlawfully discriminated against because of race, subjected to harassment related to race and or victimised, they can present a complaint to the employment tribunal. Note that an employee is a worker, but a worker is not necessarily an employee in all circumstances.

4.2 Under the Equality Act 2010, "Employment," means, "employment under a contract of employment, a contract of apprenticeship or a contract personally to do work."[96] It is the last of these ("a contract personally to do work") that has sometimes caused confusion because we tend to deem someone to be in "employment" and thus report to their "employer" under the first two - employment under a contract of employment or a contract of apprenticeship. Under the Employment Rights Act 1996, which is the major statute governing employer and employee relationship, a ""worker" (except in the phrases "shop worker" and "betting worker") means an individual who has entered into or works under (or, where the employment has ceased, worked under)—(a) a contract of employment, or (b) any other contract, whether express or implied and (if it is express) whether oral or in writing, whereby the individual undertakes to do or perform personally any work or services for another party to the contract whose status is not by virtue of the contract that

---

[96] s83(2)(a) of the Equality Act 2010

of a client or customer of any profession or business undertaking carried on by the individual."[97] Furthermore, under the 1996 Act, ""employer", in relation to an employee or a worker, means the person by whom the employee or worker is (or, where the employment has ceased, was) employed,"[98] and, "employment"—(a) in relation to an employee, means... employment under a contract of employment, and (b) in relation to a worker, means employment under his contract; and "employed" shall be construed accordingly."[99] The National Minimum Wage Act 1998 mirrors the 1996 Act[100] and Working Time Regulations 1998.[101] "It is thus possible for a person to be "employed" for the purposes of the Equality Act 2010 even though [they are] not an "employee" within the meaning of section 230 of the Employment Rights Act 1996,"[102] Therefore, it is important that a claimant refers specifically to the definition contained within the Equality Act 2010 and not those contained within the Employment Rights Act 1996, the National Minimum Wage Act 1998 and or the Working Time Regulations 1998.

---

[97] s230(3) of the Employment Rights Act 1996
[98] s230(4) of the Employment Rights Act 1996
[99] s230(5) of the Employment Rights Act 1996
[100] s54. (https://www.legislation.gov.uk/ukpga/1998/39/section/54)
[101] reg2(1) (https://www.legislation.gov.uk/uksi/1998/1833/regulation/2)
[102] Employment Judge Holbrook in *Law v Wirral Golf Club (Preliminary Hearing), para. 32*
(https://assets.publishing.service.gov.uk/media/591c3910e5274a5e51000
014/Mr_A_Law_v_Wirral_Golf_Club_Ltd_24052732016_Preliminary.p
df)

Notify ACAS

4.3 In order for the employment tribunal to hear a complaint, the Claimant must first have notified ACAS. The purpose of notifying ACAS is to see whether the parties can settle matters between them without their dispute involving the employment tribunal. Following the claimant's notification, ACAS will contact them to discuss their case and to ascertain the remedy sought. ACAS will then contact the other party or parties to see whether the matter can be resolved. The conciliatory period is for one month, although it can be extended by a maximum of a further two weeks if the parties both agree and if they feel that there is a real chance that the dispute can be resolved between them. As the purpose of notifying ACAS is to see whether the matter can be resolved accordingly, if either party believes the exercise to be fruitless, they can at any stage bring this process to an end. At this point ACAS must issue a certificate, which enables the claimant to issue their complaint in the employment tribunal if they still desire to do so. It is important to note that a claimant may decide from the outset not to conciliate and therefore elect not to engage in seeking to settle matters with the other side in which case they can request a certificate at the same time as notifying ACAS. The next stage will be to write the complaint, but before we discuss this, there are time issues to observe. Clock stop…

Time limits

4.4 Generally, a complainant must notify ACAS within three months from the date of the unlawful discriminatory act, act of harassment and or act of victimisation. If the complaint is presented outside this period then the tribunal is unlikely to have jurisdiction to hear the complaint. Note that one day late is still late and the complaint is unlikely to be heard. The best approach is not to treat the last day of the three months as a target. As soon as one finds themselves in a position to present one's complaint, they should do it immediately rather than delay it. There are, however, exceptional cases where the employment tribunal will hear a complaint presented outside the three months' period if it thinks it is just and equitable to do so. Furthermore, if the conduct in question is one that extends over a period, which we frequently term, "a continuing act," the conduct is to be treated as done at the end of the period. For example, if a conduct/act started on 1 January and continued/was extended to 15 January, the three months limitation period begins on 15 January not 1 January. However, it is important to distinguish between a continuing act and a single act with continuing consequences. The hurt feelings from a single act of harassment on, say, 1 January may well continue from and beyond the date of the conduct itself, but it is still only one conduct. This would be an example of a single act/conduct (1 January) with continuing consequences (hurt feelings), so the three months start from 1 January. Contrast this with someone being harassed on a daily basis by their manager that started on 1 January and stopped on 15 January when the manager went on holiday.

This is an example of a continuing act/conduct extending over a period of time, being 1-15 January, so the three months starts from 15 January.

Three months less 1 day

4.5   As I say, the last day of the three months is not a target to aim for. However, it is nevertheless important that one understands when the three months' period expires.

4.6   So, in a case where X believes she was overlooked for promotion on 1 January, she has a 3 month period within which to present (notify ACAS of) her complaint to the employment tribunal, otherwise she would be time-barred (for the sake of making this point I shall put aside that 'notifying' ACAS within this period is a *must* along with the extended time resulting from any conciliation period). Naturally, she thinks 3 months from 1 January is 1 April. After all, on 1 April, she will recollect that precisely 3 months to the date she was recovering from the previous evenings' New Year's Eve party on Grand Anse beach in Grenada. Furthermore, the Equality Act 2010 says, amongst other things, a, "complaint … may not be brought after the end of—(a) the period of 3 months starting with the date of the act to which the complaint relates, or (b) such other period as the employment tribunal thinks just and equitable." So, that's ok! Unfortunately, it is not. Ask those who have missed out on having their complaint heard because they are time-barred by 1 day. Yes. Late is late, whether it be by 1 day or 100 days! You see, under the Act, 3 months from 1 January is not 1 April, but 31 March. If X lodges her claim on 1 April, she will be time-barred. A simple rule of thumb to have in mind is, 'three months minus one day.' But a better rule to have in mind is not to wait until the final day to lodge your claim. Seek advice and or present your complaint well in advance of the statutory deadline!

4.7 If you decide to present a complaint in the employment tribunal, in addition to the statutory limitation period discussed before, there are other key factors to consider. Firstly, notify ACAS in good time. Do this way before the relevant limitation period expires. Secondly, name the correct party. If you fail to obtain an ACAS certificate (after notification) for the correct party then the tribunal would have no jurisdiction to hear your complaint against that 'party.' On most occasions the correct identity of the organisation/person against whom one should bring their claim is relatively straightforward. Sometimes, however, less so. For example, teachers in a maintained school – school or local authority? Also, for example, in respect of police officers, for the purposes of the Equality Act 2010, holding the office of constable is to be treated as employment—(a) by the chief officer, in respect of any act done by the chief officer in relation to a constable or appointment to the office of constable; (b) by the responsible authority, in respect of any act done by the authority in relation to a constable or appointment to the office of constable. So, does the constable present a complaint against the Chief Officer/Constable or the 'responsible authority?' If in doubt, obtain a certificate for both. It is far easier to remove the wrong party from the proceedings than it is to add the correct one!

4.8   Arguably the most important part of presenting a claim is to make sure that you present it in time as we have already discussed, plead the case that you want to plead based on the facts you believe are relevant and that you raise all the complaints. We have already discussed the first of these three, so we shall deal with the next two.

Claim Form (ET1)

4.9   The claimant presents their claim on a prescribed claim form that is known as the ET1[103]. The ET1 can be submitted online[104] or by post.[105]

4.10 All relevant information about the claimant, the respondent and the details of the complaint are to be inserted on this form, although, due to insufficient space, the details of the complaint are sometimes written on another attached document known as, "Grounds of Complaint." Among other things, in addition to the details of the complaint, the related ACAS certificate for each (if more than one) respondent must be stated.

---

[103] https://www.gov.uk/government/publications/make-a-claim-to-an-employment-tribunal-form-et1
[104] https://www.employmenttribunals.service.gov.uk/apply
[105] The addresses of the Central Offices to send a claim by post are: (1) Employment Tribunal Central Office (England and Wales) PO Box 10218, Leicester LE1 8EG, and (2) Employment Tribunals Central Office Scotland PO Box 27105 Glasgow G2 9JR

4.11　It is fair to say that the ET1 is not perfect and does not reflect the array of complaints that one can present at the employment tribunal. For example, regarding the areas we have been discussing in this book (direct discrimination, indirect discrimination, harassment and victimisation), the claim form expressly refers only to, "I was discriminated against on the grounds of race." This is done by, "indicate the **type of claim** you are making by ticking one or more of the boxes," and refers to language that reflects closer, in part, to the Race Relations Act 1976 (as amended)[106], referring to 'grounds' in place of 'because of.' There is no specific reference to the type of unlawful race discrimination - direct or indirect - and no reference at all to harassment and victimisation. These omissions have led to many problems for the layperson. If there are no detached grounds of complaint, it is left to the claimant to detail their complaint in the box, which they would also need to tick, "I am making **another type of claim** which the Employment Tribunal can deal with," which means that the claimant will need to be aware of other types of claims that they could bring but which are not specifically referred to in the ET1. Having decided on the 'type' of claim they are making, the claimant is then directed to, "state the **nature** of the claim," and is assisted by and informed that, "Examples are provided in the Guidance (Form T420)."[107] The adoption of **type** and **nature** often causes confusion, especially when viewed against the next section that asks that the claimant,

---

[106] s.1 Race Relations Act 1976 (as amended)
[107] https://assets.publishing.service.gov.uk/government/uploads/system/uploads/attachment_data/file/991138/t420-eng.pdf

"set out the background and details of your claim." However, importantly, it makes clear that, "The details of your claim should include **the date(s) when the event(s) you are complaining about happened**." The claim needs to be clear so that the respondents know the case against them and the case they have to meet and address.

Response (ET3)

4.12 Once the ET1 and notice of the claim have been sent to the respondent or respondents, it is *their*, "responsibility," to ensure that the tribunal office receives their response within the relevant time limit, being 28 days from the date that the employment tribunal *sent* the ET1, as opposed to the date *received* by the respondent(s). The prescribed form on which they detail their full response is known as the ET3[108], which contains their Grounds of Resistance. As with the ET1, the ET3 has a corresponding Guidance (Form T423)[109]. The response will not be accepted by the tribunal office unless it is on the prescribed form, which is available in the paper copy that was sent to the respondent(s) or a version of the response that can be found on the HM Courts & Tribunals Service's website.[110]

---

[108] https://assets.publishing.service.gov.uk/government/uploads/system/uploads/attachment_data/file/961374/et3-eng.pdf
[109] https://assets.publishing.service.gov.uk/government/uploads/system/uploads/attachment_data/file/950246/t423-eng.pdf
[110] www.gov.uk/being-taken-to-employment-tribunal-by-employee/overview

4.13 The respondent(s) must tick whether they, "defend the claim," which can be somewhat confusing if they defend only *part* of the claim. For example, in theory at least, they may deny direct discrimination but accept indirect discrimination or deny victimisation but accept harassment. Following this exercise, they must set out the facts on which they rely to defend the claim. The respondent needs to address the claim fully, so as to be clear to the claimant and the tribunal. If there are parts of the claim that are incomplete the respondent would need to request further and better particulars. For example, if the claim alleges that the claimant was harassed on 1 January, but no more, the respondent would need to know by whom and the details of the unwanted conduct etc. Similarly, if the claimant alleged that they were victimised on 1 February by detailing the detriment but no more, the respondent would need to know the details of the protected act on which the claimant relies. In this case, the respondent ought to raise these points in its Grounds of Resistance and reserve its rights to amend them upon its receipt of the answers contained in the request for further and better particulars.

4.14 It is strongly advised that respondents understand what it is they are defending or accepting. For example, if it is a case of indirect discrimination there is no benefit whatsoever in arguing that the claimant was not treated less favourably than another colleague because the issue of less favourable treatment is irrelevant. We shall deal with this under the next heading, "Pleadings."

Pleadings

4.15 We shall deal with various examples of what pleadings look like in Chapter Five. In the meantime, I'll explain what one needs to take into account when one is bringing a claim. However, before we get there, I need to get a little bit technical, which ought to make the understanding of this next piece a little easier.

4.16 Firstly, is what we call a head of claim. The four relevant heads of claim for the context of this discussion would be an allegation of direct discrimination, indirect discrimination, harassment and victimisation. It is important that a claimant thinks along these lines because it will help them to focus on the specific complaint they are raising and the evidence on which they shall rely to prove the case. It would also help the claimant to detail the relevant parts in order to demonstrate to the employment tribunal why they believe they have a case under the chosen heads of claim. It is sometimes confusing when a claimant mixes too much background with the actual relevant evidence that is needed to support why they believe they have a case. For example, a party may wish to detail, as background, every hint of possible discrimination (about which no complaint was raised at the material time) going back many years simply to seek to demonstrate corroboratively that the current alleged discriminatory act must therefore be true or has been proven.

4.17 It is advisable before one puts pen to paper to read the elements that make up a claim. I am not inviting a layperson to act as a lawyer but just so that the pleadings are focused on what the tribunal needs to determine. However, one is not supposed to seek to fit the facts into law but to apply the law to the facts. In this sense, the facts are fixed because they either happened or didn't. It is important to bear this in mind because the tribunal applies the law to the facts whether they are drafted by a layperson or by a lawyer. The tribunal will not be sympathetic to the former's case and apply the law incorrectly simply because the former happened to plead the case themselves. I shall now look at the four heads of claim that we have been discussing throughout this book and discuss what parties should consider when deciding to make or defend a claim.

Direct discrimination (Claimant)

4.18 In the case of direct discrimination because of race, it is necessary for the claimant to prove that they have been treated less favourably than their chosen comparator (named person) or hypothetical comparator because of the part of race relied upon. So, for example, if the claimant, a Kittitian, believes that she was treated less favourably than a colleague, a Nevisian, she would have to set out her case by detailing the less favourable treatment on which she relies. For example, she was not given a pay rise whilst her comparator was or that her comparator was promoted over her. It is fair to say that not everyone will be treated equally on everything. Therefore, it would be beneficial and helpful both to the respondent and tribunal for the claimant not only to state what did or did not happen, but, if necessary, to state why it should have been different. For example, the claimant in this case might say that she too deserved a pay rise because she worked just as hard as or harder than the comparator. Or that she should have been promoted rather than her comparator because she is more experienced and or better qualified than her.

Direct discrimination (Respondent)

4.19 It is rare that a claim does not raise issues that on the face of it, in the absence of an explanation from the respondents, there appears to be some form of less favourable treatment. Of course, if there is no less favourable treatment, the response is straightforward. But this must be addressed and brought to the attention of the claimant and tribunal. One does not leave it for the evidence at court to reveal their true case, especially if to reveal it on time could have brought the case to an end earlier. For example, if the respondent can show that our Nevisian comparator was not given a pay rise at all or that she was given a pay rise to match the pay of the claimant's (because both, "worked just as hard," and was thus previously underpaid), there would appear to be *no* less favourable treatment for our Kittitian claimant, and this should be stated in the Grounds of Resistance. A tribunal would not be happy for this to be revealed late in the process after much *unnecessary* expense has been incurred and time expended by both parties. Of course, there may well be less favourable treatment but not because of race. If that is the case, the respondents should state what the less favourable treatment *was* based on. Simply stating that the less favourable treatment was not because of race without more will not suffice.

Indirect discrimination (Claimant)

4.20 Regarding indirect discrimination, it is important that the claimant identifies the correct PCP that is applicable and, therefore, upon which ought properly to be relied. Before one does that it is advisable that one considers the various parts to the claim, which might later lead to a honing of the PCP. In other words, it identifies the particular disadvantage and then identifies the relevant, related, PCP if at all there is one. Take, for example, a situation where a respondent required its staff to take and pass a generic test, irrespective of its direct relevance to the position in question, before being eligible for promotion. A higher proportion of staff from a particular race failed when compared with those not of the particular race. Therefore, in this case, it is unlikely to be productive for a claimant to focus on the time of day or the day of the week the test is set when, on the face it, the focus might properly be on the PCP to have to pass the generic test in the first place. So, for example, the sitting and passing of the generic test was applied or would have applied to *persons* who do not share the claimant's race. Having established this application, the claimant would then need to show that the PCP had put, or would have put, *persons* with whom the claimant *does* share their race at a particular disadvantage when compared with *persons* with whom they do not. Note it is important that we approach each part systematically. At this juncture, the focus is on the two *classes* of *persons* – 'those with whom the claimant *does* share her/his race,' and 'those with whom the claimant *does not* share her/his race.' In other words, those who share the claimant's race are put or would be put at the *particular disadvantage* (*not* being promoted because they failed the generic test) when compared to those who do not (who *are* promoted because they passed the generic test).

4.21 Having identified the said *persons* and the groups to which they belong (persons who do and persons who do not share the claimant's race), the claimant, *personally*, enters the equation with the question whether the PCP *itself* had put or would have put her/him at the particular disadvantage. In other words, did she fail the generic test or was likely to fail it because of what we established in the previous steps, in that those with whom she shares her race were put or would have been put at the particular disadvantage of failing the generic test and, therefore, missing out on promotion? A sound argument for the claimant could be to frame it as follows. A class of X is likely to fail Y. Z is of the class of X. Therefore, Z is likely to fail Y. If all the previous steps are in the claimant's favour, so to speak, she will succeed in her claim if the respondent cannot show the PCP to be a proportionate means of achieving a legitimate aim. In other words, for example, the claimant demonstrates that the sitting and passing of the generic test was a disproportionate means to achieving the legitimate aim of giving staff the opportunity of promotion.

Indirect discrimination (Respondent)

4.22 Putting aside a challenge as to whether the claimant 'shares the race' of the persons said to be put or would be put at the particular disadvantage (i.e. the claimant is Guyanese but the disadvantaged class is Tobagan), the question for the respondent to address is whether there was a PCP. If there was no PCP then that ought to be the end of that part of the response. However, as shall be touched on under *Pleadings* in Chapter Five, it is always good to deal with the allegations in their entirety in case the employment tribunal does not agree or accept part of the response or the evidence unfolds in a previously unforeseeable/unpredictable way. So, for example, the respondent may wish to plead 'in the alternative' that in the event that the employment tribunal does not agree with the respondent that there was no PCP as alleged by the claimant, what its position is. It would be an *artificial* response but necessary. For example, if the response says there was no PCP then, taking the steps systematically as discussed above with the claim, it would seem peculiar to the respondent to state, however, *had there been* the alleged PCP it did not put, or would not put, persons with whom the claimant shares her race at a particular disadvantage when compared with persons with whom the claimant does not share it. To add to the peculiarity, this *alternative* exercise should be repeated throughout. So, having said the last, the respondent should state its position if the tribunal does not agree with it *again*. In this case, the respondent would deal with whether the PCP put, or would put, the claimant at that disadvantage. Then, finally, the respondent will deal with whether the PCP (which it as already stated did not exist) was justified.

4.23 The above, of course, deals with a situation where the respondent denies the PCP. However, there are many permutations where the existence of the PCP as alleged is not fatal to the respondent. For example, the respondent may admit various elements, but deny that the PCP applied to the claimant or, if it did, it was justified in that it can show it to be a proportionate means of achieving a legitimate aim.

Harassment (Claimant)

4.24 With harassment, the first challenge for the claimant is to show that the conduct in question was unwanted. It ought not to be too difficult for the claimant to say why they say the conduct was unwanted by them, especially as, "Unwanted conduct covers a wide range of behaviour, including spoken or written words or abuse, imagery, graffiti, physical gestures, facial expressions, mimicry, jokes, pranks, acts affecting a person's surroundings or other physical behaviour."[111] However, detailing the unwanted conduct is not the same as showing that the alleged harasser accepted that the conduct was unwanted and that it was related to race. Therefore, it would assist the tribunal if the claimant were to state why the alleged harasser knew or ought to have known that such conduct was unwanted. For example, the harasser ought to know that saying something

---

[111] Equality Act 2010 Code of Practice, Para 7.7

offensive about the claimant's race in the workplace within the earshot of the claimant is likely to be a conduct unwanted by the claimant.

4.25 Having given details of the unwanted conduct, the claimant then details either *purpose* or *effect*. Note that the claimant does not need to show both. Alleging the first necessarily involves examining the harasser's motives or intent. However, note that what we are examining is, "the **conduct** has the **purpose**." The claimant will then seek to adduce evidence that supports the allegation that the alleged harasser intended the conduct to have the purpose of violating their dignity or creating an intimidating, hostile, degrading, humiliating or offensive environment for them. The question of whether the purpose of the conduct had the intended effect is irrelevant. In other words, for example, it would not assist the harasser to say that the purpose of saying something offensive about the claimant's race was to violate the claimant's dignity, but the purpose was not fulfilled because the claimant is clearly, "thick skinned and took it on the chin!"

4.26 Arguably, the easier approach is to focus on the effect of the conduct and is probably the one most relied on. In this case, the focus is on the *object* of the conduct. Again, the claimant ought not to have much difficulty stating why they say the unwanted conduct violated their dignity, or created an intimidating, hostile, degrading, humiliating or offensive environment for them. However, the claimant is not the sole judge of whether the unwanted conduct has the alleged effect. As discussed previously, there are subjective and objective factors together with the other circumstances of the case to be considered. Even then, according to the EAT, "not every racially slanted adverse comment or conduct may constitute the violation of a person's dignity. Dignity is not necessarily violated by things said or done which are trivial or transitory, particularly if it should have been clear that any offence was unintended. While it is very important that employers, and tribunals, are sensitive to the hurt that can be caused by racially offensive comments or conduct (or indeed comments or conduct on other grounds covered by the cognate legislation to which we have referred), it is also important not to encourage a culture of hypersensitivity or the imposition of legal liability in respect of every unfortunate phrase."[112]

Harassment (Respondent)

4.27 The first thing to address for the alleged harasser is the unwanted conduct *related to* race. There are four main parts to this. Firstly, the respondent could deny that any such conduct occurred. Secondly, if it did occur, the conduct was not unwanted because, maybe, the claimant actively engaged in the conduct and, "gave as good as he got!" Thirdly, the conduct is admitted but it is denied that it was related to race. Fourthly, as discussed before, the context might give a better understanding of the conduct that may suggest that the conduct was not related to race. It would therefore be

---

[112] *Richmond Pharmacology v Dhaliwal [2009] ICR 724*

for the respondent to explain in which light it believes the conduct should be viewed.

4.28 For reasons already discussed, it may well be easier for the alleged harasser to defend a claim based on the conduct's *purpose* rather than its *effect*. Regarding the latter, therefore, the alleged harasser would have to detail, with examples where possible, why they believe that, taking into account the circumstances of the matter and whether it is reasonable for the conduct to have that effect, even if the complainant was genuinely upset by it. "Tribunals must not cheapen the significance," of the words *violating* the claimant's dignity, or *creating* an *intimidating, hostile, degrading, humiliating* or *offensive* environment for them. "They are an important control to prevent trivial acts causing minor upsets being caught by the concept of harassment."[113]

Victimisation (Claimant)

4.29 The ET1, "does not identify a protected act in the true legal sense merely by making a reference to a criticism, grievance or complaint without suggesting that the criticism, grievance or complaint was in some sense an allegation of discrimination or otherwise a contravention of the legislation."[114] Simply stating that one had been discriminated against without reference to race, on which a

---

[113] *Grant (appellant) v. HM Land Registry (respondent) and Equality and Human Rights Commission (interverner) - [2011] IRLR 748, para. 47*
[114] *Beneviste v Kingston University [2006] UKEAT/0393/05*

claimant later sought to rely, was held not to be a protected act.[115]

4.29.1 In a recent case, the claimant was held to have been victimised by the respondent when it failed to investigate his grievances, which had referred to allegations of race discrimination and therefore to alleged breaches of the Equality Act 2010. "It was sufficient, as a matter of law, that the failure to investigate the grievances was 'materially influenced by the fact that the Grievances raised allegations of discrimination.'"[116]

4.30 Unlike the others we have discussed – direct and indirect discrimination and harassment – the *act* complained of is not *necessarily* because of a link to a protected characteristic but, rather, one linked to a protected act. The focus here is on the protected act *and* the reaction to it. Once the claimant details the relevant part of the protected act – written or orally – on which they rely, they then need to show the reaction to it and why; *cause* (protected act) and *effect* (detriment). For example, the claimant was denied promotion because he supported and accompanied a colleague who had raised a grievance, alleging that her manager had racially harassed her. In this case, it is irrelevant whether the grievance was upheld, the focus for the claimant is that the employer did not take kindly to his supporting and accompanying her as, "he should have

---

[115] *Durrani v London Borough of Ealing* UKEAT/0454/2012/RN, *(Transcript)*
[116] *Iwuchukwu v City Hospitals Sunderland NHS Foundation Trust* [2019] IRLR 1022; [2019] EWCA Civ 498

known better," and, therefore, treated him detrimentally because of it. Therefore, "detrimentally," in this context, is not, as we see with direct discrimination, based on the principle of *less favourable* treatment but on *unfavourable* treatment *because* he did the protected act of supporting and accompanying the colleague. Detriment is widely adopted, in that, "Generally, a detriment is anything which the individual concerned might reasonably consider changed their position for the worse or put them at a disadvantage. This could include being rejected for promotion, denied an opportunity to represent the organisation at external events, excluded from opportunities to train, or overlooked in the allocation of discretionary bonuses or performance-related awards."[117]

Victimisation (Respondent)

4.31 It is unsurprising why so many victimisation complaints succeed because people are often deemed to be reacting to the nature of the protected act rather than *necessarily* their having been accused of, for example, breaching the Equality Act 2010 themselves. For example, a colleague accuses the Managing Director of direct race discrimination. His colleagues take grave offence to that because they see it as unmeritorious and, therefore, they all shun him by not inviting him to key meetings, out for company social gatherings, leave him out of key emails about the company etc. Ironically, the person against whom a complaint was

---

[117] Equality Act 2010 Code of Practice, para. 9.8

made that gave rise to the protected act may not even be the person alleged to have victimised the claimant.

4.32 Another difficulty sometimes confronted by the respondent is that the protected act has no expiry date because, effectively, it is *the reaction to it* that gives rise to a claim. Therefore, a protected act could have been many weeks, months or years before the act of victimisation on which the claimant relies occurred. Of course, the greater the period between the protected act and alleged act of the victimisation the harder it may also be for the claimant to prove cause and effect between the two.

4.33 Therefore, the two parts to attack are either (or both) that the alleged protected act on which the claimant relies is not a true protected act in that it does not assert *facts capable of amounting to such in law* or that the treatment on which the claimant relies as the act of victimisation did not happen, did happen but was not because of the alleged protected act or did happen but was not, in any event, a detriment.

Employer's liability

4.34 The employer is vicariously liable for anything done by an employee in the course of their employment and anything done by an agent for the employer, with the authority of the employer, must be treated as also done by the employer. Crucially, it does not matter whether that thing is done with the employer's knowledge or approval. Liability also extends to aiding, causing, instructing or inducing their employees or agents to commit an unlawful act. Take note that an employer will still be liable for discrimination or harassment of former workers if the discrimination or harassment arises out of and is closely connected to a relationship covered by the Equality Act 2010 that has ended.[118] For example, the giving of an untrue and inaccurate reference for a former employee because of race would be caught by the Equality Act 2010 and give the claimant a claim.

Statutory Defence

4.35 However, in proceedings against the employer in respect of anything alleged to have been done by the employee in the course of their employment, it is a defence for the employer to show that it took all reasonable steps to prevent the employee from doing that thing or from doing anything of that description.

4.36 "An employer would be considered to have taken all reasonable steps if there were no further steps that they could have been expected to take. In deciding whether a step is reasonable, an employer should consider its likely effect and whether an alternative step could be more effective. However, a step does not have to be effective to be reasonable."[119] Examples of 'reasonable steps' are given in the Equality Act 2010 Code of Practice as, "implementing an equality policy; ensuring workers are aware of the policy; providing equal opportunities training; reviewing the equality policy as appropriate; and dealing

---

[118] s.108 of the Equality Act 2010
[119] Equality Act 2010 Code of Practice, para. 10.51

effectively with employee complaints."[120] However, "it is important to bear in mind that the Code of Practice is not to be considered in this regard as comprising a list of statutory requirements, each of which must be met in order for an employer to be regarded as having taken all reasonable steps. The steps that would be reasonable in a particular case would depend on the facts. Moreover, the Code of Practice suggests that the reasonable steps 'might' include those set out; it does not suggest that the failure to take any one of those steps in relation to any policy will necessarily mean that the reasonable steps defence under s. 109(4) of the [Equality Act 2010] cannot succeed."[121] Therefore, a claimant, relying on these examples, appealed unsuccessfully to the EAT, submitting that the employment tribunal, having found that there was no evidence that the company took steps to publicise, audit or monitor its policies, was not entitled to conclude that the company had taken all reasonable steps to prevent the discriminatory act.[122] In this case, the EAT held that, "the Tribunal regarded as significant that the employer treated [the harasser's] conduct seriously and gave her a final written warning. The Tribunal was, in our judgement, entitled in those circumstances to conclude that, notwithstanding the absence of any evidence as to the publication, auditing or monitoring of the policy, the Respondent did take reasonable steps to prevent its employees from doing the discriminatory act in question."[123]

---

[120] Equality Act 2010 Code of Practice, para. 10.52
[121] *Forbes (appellant) v LHR Airport Ltd (respondent) [2019] IRLR 890, para. 51*
[122] *Forbes (appellant) v LHR Airport Ltd (respondent) [2019] IRLR 890*
[123] *Forbes (appellant) v LHR Airport Ltd (respondent) [2019] IRLR 890,*

Territorial Jurisdiction

4.37 An employee must have sufficient connection with Britain to be protected under the Equality Act 2010 and, thus, for the employment tribunal to have jurisdiction to hear their complaint under the 2010 Act (discrimination, harassment, victimisation etc.). Regarding work, there is no territorial boundaries expressed within the 2010 Act, however, "It is inconceivable that Parliament was intending to confer rights upon employees working in foreign countries and having no connection with Great Britain."[124] But the 2010 Act, "leaves it to tribunals to determine whether the law applies, depending for example on the connection between the employment relationship and Great Britain."[125] Notwithstanding this, however, ordinarily, the question on whether the employee has sufficient connection with Britain should simply be whether they are working in Great Britain at the time when, for example, they were dismissed.[126]

Jurisdiction – discrimination by non-employers

4.38 With limited exceptions, it is plainly obvious that an employee or former employee will be the claimant and that an employer or former employer will be the respondent. To some, it is less obvious when a worker is

---

para. 52
[124] *Lawson (appellant) v. Serco Ltd (respondents); Botham (appellant) v. Ministry of Defence (respondents); Crofts and others (respondents) v. Veta Ltd and others (appellants) [2006] IRLR 289*
[125] Equality Act 2010 Explanatory Note 15 (https://www.legislation.gov.uk/ukpga/2010/15/notes/division/2/3/1)
[126] *Lawson (appellant) v. Serco Ltd) [2006] IRLR 289, para 27*

not an employee under a contract of employment (contract of service) but in 'employment' under, 'a contract personally to do work.'[127] To some, it is *even* less obvious when one is a contract worker.[128] And, to some, it becomes very confusing when it is plainly obvious that the relationship between the parties does not fit comfortably within any of the above and yet the arbiter of a dispute between them is the employment tribunal. For example, an employment tribunal does not appear to be the obvious place to hear a dispute between a claimant and the governing body of their profession. But it can and does arise.

4.39 We know that the employment tribunal has jurisdiction to determine a complaint relating to a person's work.[129] 'Qualification bodies' *must not*, amongst other things, unlawfully discriminate, harass or victimise a person on stipulated grounds.[130] However, if they were to do so (unlawfully discriminate, harass or victimise a person), would or could such an act be said 'to relate' to a person's work, thus potentially bringing a complaint on those grounds within the jurisdiction of the employment tribunal?

4.40 In a recent case,[131] following the dismissal of the claimant doctor by her employer whom she had taken successfully

---

[127] s83(2)(a) of the Equality Act 2010
[128] s41 of the Equality Act 2010
[129] s120(1)(a) of the Equality Act 2010
[130] s53 of the Equality Act 2010
[131] *Michalak (respondent) v General Medical Council and others*

to the employment tribunal, in that, 'The tribunal found that her dismissal had been unfair and contaminated by sex and race discrimination and victimisation,' the respondent employer reported her to the General Medical Council (GMC). They reported her *post* dismissal but *prior to* the tribunal's said judgment. The claimant was not deregistered, but she presented a complaint to the employment tribunal, alleging a series of claims of discrimination on the part of the GMC that related to the manner in which it pursued its fitness to practise application and its failure to investigate her complaints against other doctors in the trust where she had been employed and, like I said, which had been found to have, amongst other things, discriminated against and victimised the claimant etc.

4.41 There was no statutory appeal available to the claimant to pursue her complaints against the GMC. However, the GMC applied for her complaints to be struck out on the grounds that the employment tribunal did not have jurisdiction to hear her claim, and that, in general, the route available to her was to seek leave for judicial review. However, the Supreme Court held that the employment *did* have jurisdiction to hear her claim as it *related to her work*. It held that judicial review in the context of this case was not in the nature of an appeal and neither was it a remedy provided by reason of an enactment.

(appellants) [2018] IRLR 60; [2018] ICR 49; [2017] UKSC 71; [2018] 1 All ER 463; [2017] 1 WLR 4193

~ CHAPTER FIVE ~

"A great deal has changed in the decade since the introduction of the first Race Relations Bill in 1965"

Mr Roy Jenkins[132]

---

[132] 4 March 1976, House of Commons

PLEADINGS

5.1 Now that we have what needs to go into our claim and response, we look at form. I should make it clear that there is nothing wrong with writing a claim or response in a narrative form. What is important is that the case for each side is put clearly and deals with the various parts that are needed either successfully to win the claim or to defend the action. I am of the view that the simpler the language adopted the better. Pleadings do not have to read like a merger contract between two large shipping companies! Importantly, there is no one correct way to plead. The following, for example, could take numerous forms. One simply needs to express clearly their case.

5.2 *Scenario 1*

Delroy and John worked for a firm of Chartered Surveyors. John was allowed to attend a day release degree course, which was not offered to Delroy. Delroy brings a claim.

5.3 *Claim 1 (Delroy) – Grounds of Complaint (Claimant)*

1. The Claimant is white. He has been employed by the Respondent as a junior surveyor since 7 January 2019.

2. The Respondent is a firm of Chartered Surveyors in Bristol, currently employing 15 surveyors of which 5 are ranked as junior surveyors, which includes the Claimant.

3. The Claimant asked the Respondent to attend a day release degree course and was refused on the basis that the covid pandemic had meant that the firm had made a loss and there was now a freeze on the training budget.

4. On or around 1 March 2021 Mr. John YY, who is black, joined the Respondent as a junior surveyor and undertook the same surveying duties as the Claimant and the other junior surveyors. In April 2021 the Claimant discovered that Mr. John YY was allowed to attend on a day release degree course.

5. The Claimant disputes the Respondent's explanation about a freeze on the training budget because Mr. John YY's course must have been budgeted for by the Respondent to allow him to attend. The Claimant contends that he was treated less favourably than Mr. John YY because of his race, being his colour, by the Respondent's refusal to offer him the same training opportunity as it did to Mr. John YY.

6. The Claimant claims:

   (i) a declaration that the Respondent unlawfully discriminated against him because of his colour;

   (ii) a recommendation that the Respondent take such action to allow him the attend his surveying course;

    (iii)   compensation.

5.4 *Grounds of Resistance to Claim 1 (Respondent)*

1. The Respondent denies that it discriminated against the Claimant because of his race, being, as he stated, his colour, as alleged by him or at all. References to paragraphs are to those contained within the Grounds of Complaint.

2. Paragraphs 1 and 2 are admitted.

3. Save that it is admitted that due to the covid pandemic the firm had made a loss and there was a freeze on the training budget para 3 is denied. The Claimant's supervisor is Ms. Julia MM and she has no record or details of any such request having been made by the Claimant. Furthermore, the Claimant is asked to provide further and better particulars of:

    (a) Whom did he ask to attend the course?
    (b) What precisely was said between him and the person whom he asked?
    (c) When did this conversation take place?

4. Notwithstanding the last, on 1 February 2021 Mr. John YY accepted an offer to join the Respondent as a junior surveyor. In 2020 he had been offered a place at BB University to study one day a week on its surveying degree course. The course was paid for in

advance by his previous employer. However, due to the covid pandemic and national lockdown the course was postponed to September 2021. It was on this basis that Mr. John YY was allowed to attend his course, which, as already stated, was paid for not by the Respondent but by his previous employer.

5. Save that the Respondent does not admit when the Claimant discovered that Mr. John YY was allowed to attend a day release degree course paragraph 4 is admitted.

6. Regarding paragraph 5, it is denied that the Respondent treated the Claimant less favourably than his named comparator, Mr. John YY, because of his race, being his colour, by refusing to offer him the same training opportunity as it did to Mr. John YY as alleged by the Claimant or at all.

7. In consequence, the Claimant is not entitled to the declaration, recommendation and or compensation sought.

5.5 *Scenario 2*

A firm of Chartered Accountants had been concerned about its lack of diversity and embarked on a campaign to address this by both advertising wider than in its local vicinity and using media with a more diverse audience. Following a successful recruitment campaign in 2017, it recruited its first non-English members of staff since its formation 29 years ago, being five of Indian nation origins. The twelve remaining Chartered Accountants were all English. In 2021 the firm decided to change its company pension scheme to less attractive terms, but this would not be applicable to those who had been at the firm for 5 years or longer. The Claimants do not believe this to be an act of direct discrimination.

5.6 *Claim 2 (One & Others) – Grounds of Complaint (Claimant)*

1. On 5 June 2017 the Claimants, who are all of Indian national origin, commenced working for the Respondent as Chartered Accountants. Of the Respondent's seventeen Chartered Accountants, twelve were English.

2. At the time of joining the Respondent all staff were on a lucrative defined benefit scheme (DBS). On 1 June 2021 the Respondent introduced a change in the pension scheme to a less attractive defined contribution scheme (DCS). However, those members of staff who had worked at the Respondent for 5 years or longer had a choice to remain in the DBS.

3. The Claimants all began working for the Respondent four years ago and therefore cannot meet the criterion or provision set by the Respondent that would enable them to have the option of remaining in the lucrative DBS.

4. The Respondent discriminated against the Claimants by applying the criterion and or provision to them, being if the accountants (a) have less than five years employment with the Respondent they must switch from the DBS to the DCS or (b) have at least five years employment with the Respondent so they have an option to remain in the DBS (PCPs), which are discriminatory in relation to Claimants' relevant protected characteristic, being their Indian origin.

5. The Claimants accept that the Respondent applied the PCPs to all accountants. However, the PCPs put or would put accountants of Indian origin at a particular disadvantage when compared with accountants who are not. In consequence, the PCPs put the Claimants at that disadvantage, and the Claimants contend that the Respondent cannot show the PCPs to be a proportionate means of achieving a legitimate aim.

6. The Claimants claim:

   (i) a declaration that the Respondent unlawfully discriminated against them because of their Indian origin;

   (ii) a recommendation that the Respondent take such action to allow them to remain in the DBS, and that the partners attend training on anti-discrimination and Equal Opportunities;

(iii) compensation.

5.7 *Grounds of Resistance to Claim 2 (Respondent)*

1. The Respondent is an equal opportunities employer and its partners attend anti-discrimination and diversity awareness & inclusion courses once every two years. In fact, four years ago the Respondent had been concerned about the lack of diversity within the firm and embarked on a campaign to address this underrepresentation. As a result of this successful campaign the Respondent is happy to say the Claimants were employed.

2. References hereinafter are to the Grounds of Complaint.

3. The Claimants bring a claim of indirect discrimination because of their Indian origin, which the Respondent denies it did.

4. Paragraph 1 is admitted.

5. Save that it is denied that at the time of joining the Respondent all staff were on a lucrative defined benefit scheme paragraph 2 is admitted.

6. Paragraph 3 is admitted. However, the Respondent had to have a cut-off point and applied the criterion and or provision accordingly.

7. Paragraph 4 is denied. It is the Respondent's position that the correct pool for the PCP should be limited only to staff with fewer than five years continuous employment with the Respondent. In this case, there would be no particular disadvantage to the Claimants.

8. Save that it is admitted that the Respondent applied the PCPs to all accountants, paragraph 5 is denied.

9. During a partners' meeting in February 2021 it was agreed that the Respondent would replace the DBS with the DCS for all staff. The decision was influenced by a report from the trustees of the DBS who reported that it was financially unsustainable and could potentially put the Respondent in a position where it would be unable to fulfil its obligations under the DBS. The Respondent looked to a point when it had fewer employees and used this to gauge the cut-off of five years.

10. In the event that the tribunal accepts the PCPs to be correct, in light of the above, the Respondent contends that the PCPs were a proportionate means of achieving the legitimate aim of enabling it to be able to fulfil its obligations under the DBS.

5.8 *Scenario 3*

A pharmaceutical company hosted a work function. Drinks were free. Rachel and Phil were on the same table. Phil began telling racist jokes at which he alone on the table laughed. Rachel told Phil to stop as she found his comments quite offensive. Phil informed Rachel that as he was not talking about her or 'your kind' she should not have an issue and continued.

5.9 *Claim 3 (Rachel) – Grounds of Complaint (Claimant)*

1. The Claimant is employed by the Respondent as a sales executive.

2. The Respondent is a pharmaceutical company. On 13 December 2019 the Respondent held a function for staff, clients and customers. During the function a member of staff, Mr. Phil TT, repeatedly made racist jokes and comments such as, "XXX," "YYY," and "ZZZ." The Claimant told Mr. Phil TT to stop his conduct as she found his comments to be offensive. However, he informed her that as he was not talking about her or her 'kind' she should not have an issue and continued.

3. On 16 December 2019 the Claimant complained to her supervisor, Ms. Sylvia WW, about her being harassed by Mr. Phil TT to which Ms. Sylvia WW said that he probably had too much to drink and that the Claimant should, "loosen up a little."

4. The Claimant felt harassed pursuant to s.26 of the Equality Act 2010 in that Mr. Phil TT engaged in a

conduct unwanted by her that was related to race, and which had the purpose or effect of creating an offensive environment for her.

5. The Claimant claims:

   (i) a declaration that the Respondent unlawfully harassed her through or by conducts related to race;

   (ii) a recommendation that the Respondent's staff attend training in anti-discrimination conduct;

   (iii) compensation.

5.10 *Grounds of Resistance to Claim 3 (Respondent)*

   1. The Respondent denies that it harassed the Claimant as she alleges in the Grounds of Complaint or at all.

   2. Paragraphs 1 to 3 of the Grounds of Complaint are admitted.

   3. Save that it is not admitted how the Claimant felt paragraph 4 is denied. It is denied that the alleged conduct was unwanted by the Claimant because she had in the past engaged in conduct that some would say was bordering on racist behaviour.

4. Mr. Phil TT and the Claimant were until recently in an intimate relationship. The Claimant has now got a new boyfriend and has now become sensitive to jokes that she once found funny. Even if the conduct in question was unwanted, due to the Claimant's previous conduct, Mr. Phil TT was not made aware.

5. Alternatively, if the tribunal were to find that the conduct was unwanted by the Claimant the Respondent denies that the conduct had the purpose or effect of creating an offensive environment for her. As the Claimant had engaged in similar conduct the purpose was never to create the alleged environment. Also, as the Claimant had engaged in similar conduct previously she would not have been so sensitive as to find that the effect created an offensive environment for her.

6. Alternatively, if the tribunal were to find that the Claimant had been harassed by Mr. Phil TT as she alleges, the Respondent contends that it took all reasonable steps to prevent him from making racist jokes and or harassing others in the course of his employment or from doing anything of that description such as implementing an equality policy; ensuring workers are aware of the policy; and providing equal opportunities training.

5.11 *Scenario 4*

In June 2020 Stephanie raised a grievance that her boss, Stan PP, had discriminated against her by not furloughing her. The grievance was not upheld. On 1 April 2021 Stephanie was given notice of termination of her contract because, said the company, the leisure business had been hit hard during the national lockdown.

5.12 *Claim 4 (Stephanie) – Grounds of Complaint (Claimant)*

1. Between 2 December 2019 and 30 April 2021 the Claimant was employed by ABCD Pubs Ltd as a deputy assistant manager at one of its pubs in Leeds. In 2020 June 2020 the Claimant was forced to work despite many of her colleagues being furloughed and earning 80% of their salary for not working. In consequence, the Claimant raised a grievance against her manager, Mr. Stan PP, for discriminating against her because of her race. By raising the grievance, the Claimant made a protected act ('Protected Act').

2. Mr. Stan PP clearly took grave exception to the Protected Act and, accordingly, dismissed the Claimant by giving her one month's notice on 1 April 2021.

3. The Claimant contends that her dismissal was an act of victimisation, contrary to s.27(1)(a) and s.39(4)(c) of the Equality Act 2010.

4. The Claimant claims:

   (i) a declaration that the Respondent victimised her by dismissing her;
   (ii) compensation.

5.13 *Grounds of Resistance to Claim 4 (Respondent)*

1. The Respondent denies victimising the Claimant.

2. The Respondent owns a chain of pubs in the Yorkshire area and was forbidden from opening its pubs due to the national lockdown. In June 2020 the respondent was allowed to open some of its pubs due to having outside facilities. The Claimant was one of its many valued staff and so it required her to work rather than be furloughed.

3. The Claimant wanted to be furloughed, but the Respondent needed her at work. In consequence, she raised a grievance against her manager, Mr. Stan PP, alleging that he was, 'discriminating against me.' The grievance was not upheld.

4. The Respondent then went through a difficult trading time and suffered heavy losses. It was decided to reduce its workforce and dismiss most of its staff with less than two years continuous service, of which the Claimant was one. In consequence, on 1 April 2021

the Claimant was given one month's notice pursuant to clause 19 of her contract of employment.

5. The decision to terminate the Claimant's contract was unconnected and had nothing to do with her grievance, which the Respondent shall address further below.

6. Dealing specifically with the allegations raised in the Grounds of Complaint.

7. Save that it is denied that the Claimant raised a grievance against her manager, Mr. Stan PP, for discriminating against her because of her race, that she was 'forced to work', and that she made a protected act ('Protected Act') paragraph 1 is admitted.

8. The Claimant did not allege that the Respondent had discriminated against her because of her race. She said it was because some colleagues had been furloughed and she had not. This was the nature of the alleged discrimination. Therefore, the Respondent contends that this does not amount to a protected act and it follows that the Claimant cannot succeed in her claim of victimisation.

9. In light of the above, the Respondent is of the view that the claim should either be struck out pursuant to r.37 as having no reasonable prospect of success or that the Claimant be required to pay a deposit order

pursuant to r.39 as the claim has little reasonable prospect of success.

10. Save that it is admitted that Mr. Stan PP dismissed the Claimant by his giving her one month's notice on 1 April 2021 for reasons given in these Grounds of Resistance paragraphs 2 and 3 are denied.

11. In consequence, the claim should rightly be dismissed.

Amending the Claim

5.14 At any time up to and including during a hearing a claim can be changed or added to. This is done by the party wishing to make the change or addition to seek leave (permission) from the tribunal to amend accordingly. A party seeking such leave should have a draft of the amendment they wish the tribunal to consider and allow. Generally, the sooner an application is made to the tribunal the better the chances are of having the application for leave to amend being granted. In other words, seeking leave to amend 10 months before a substantive hearing (the trial) has a better chance of being granted — subject to matters I shall discuss below — than 10 minutes before such a hearing. Effectively, there are two types of amendments for which one would normally seek leave. One entails what is often called a 'relabelling exercise' and the other is seeking an entirely new claim. Let us take each in turn.

Relabelling Exercise

5.15 As discussed in Chapter 4, in addition to indicating, "the **type of claim** you are making by ticking one or more of the boxes,"[133] the claimant writes a narrative of their complaint/claim. Let us say that a claimant ticks the boxes under 8.1 of the ET1 that indicates that they were, "discriminated against on the grounds of", "race" and neither ticks nor makes an entry in the box that states, "I am making another type of claim which the Employment Tribunal can deal with." Let us say that upon receipt of the ET1 the Respondent files its ET3, dealing solely with direct discrimination because it had assumed that, despite the contents of the narrative that might indicate otherwise, as the claimant had not expressly stated that they were, "making another type of claim which the Employment Tribunal can deal with," there was no other type of claim besides direct discrimination because of race.

---

[133] See 4.11

5.16   Upon their receipt of the ET3 and accompanying Grounds of Resistance the claimant discovers that the respondent has addressed neither whether the grievance was a, 'protected act,'[134] nor, if it did, whether they were victimised because of it.

5.17   Immediately, the claimant seeks leave to amend their claim, seeking to persuade the tribunal that although they had not stated explicitly that they were bringing a claim of victimisation, the facts in the narrative show that they had this in mind – the claimant raised a grievance against her manager, Mr. Stan PP, for discriminating against her because of her race and believes the respondent dismissed her because of this part of her grievance. On this basis, the claimant states that victimisation is not a new claim on the facts but simply a relabelling exercise of the facts already pleaded in the narrative.

5.18   The respondent opposes the application on the basis that the claimant omitted to mention 'victimisation' on the ET1 Claim Form. The tribunal determined the issues, citing and relying on *Selkent Bus Co. Ltd v Moore*.[135]

---

[134] See 2.45-50
[135] *[1996] ICR 836*

Selkent Bus Co. Ltd v Moore (E.A.T)

5.19   Mummery J. (as he then was), delivering judgment:

> "(4) Whenever the discretion to grant an amendment is invoked, the tribunal should take into account all the circumstances and should balance the injustice and hardship of allowing the amendment against the injustice and hardship of refusing it.
>
> "(5) What are the relevant circumstances? It is impossible and undesirable to attempt to list them exhaustively, but the following are certainly relevant.
>
> (a) The nature of the amendment. Applications to amend are of many different kinds, ranging, on the one hand, from the correction of clerical and typing errors, the addition of factual details to existing allegations and the addition or substitution of other labels for facts already pleaded to, on the other hand, the making of entirely new factual allegations which change the basis of the existing claim. The tribunal have to decide whether the amendment

sought is one of the minor matters or is a substantial alteration pleading a new cause of action.

(b) The applicability of time limits. If a new complaint or cause of action is proposed to be added by way of amendment, it is essential for the tribunal to consider whether that complaint is out of time and, if so, whether the time limit should be extended under the applicable statutory provisions...

(c) The timing and manner of the application. An application should

not be refused solely because there has been a delay in making it. There are no time limits laid down in the Regulations of [2013][136] for the making of amendments. The amendments may be made at any time-before, at, even after the hearing of the case. Delay in making the application is, however, a discretionary factor. It is relevant to consider why the application was not made earlier and why it is now being made: for example, the discovery of new facts or new information appearing from

---

[136] Employment Tribunals (Constitution and Rules of Procedure) Regulations 2013 – See 9.5

documents disclosed on discovery. Whenever taking any factors into account, the paramount considerations are the relative injustice and hardship involved in refusing or granting an amendment. Questions of delay, as a result of adjournments, and additional costs, particularly if they are unlikely to be recovered by the successful party, are relevant in reaching a decision."

5.20 Returning to our scenario above,[137] the tribunal allowed the claimant's amendment on the basis that the alleged victimisation, although not stated expressly on the face of the ET1 Claim Form, amounted to an, "addition of other labels [i.e. additional to the complaint of direct discrimination because of her race] for facts already pleaded to," in the claimant's written narrative of their complaint/claim. It was clear to the tribunal that, within the narrative, the claimant was complaining that she had been subjected to a detriment (dismissal)[138] by the respondent because she did a protected act by 'making an allegation (whether or not express) that the respondent had contravened the Equality Act 2010 (raised a grievance

---

[137] 5.15-18
[138] s.27(1) Equality Act 2010

against her manager, Mr. Stan PP, for discriminating against her because of her race)[139]

Entirely New Claim

5.21 If neither the ET1 Claim Form nor the accompanying narrative indicates that the claimant is relying on a particular type of claim then an application to amend will be based on the claimant raising a new claim. For example, where, 'The Claimant contends that he was treated less favourably than Mr. John YY because of his race, being his colour, by the Respondent's refusal to offer him the same training opportunity as it did to Mr. John YY,' but makes no reference to 'victimisation' on the ET1 Claim Form or accompanying narrative/pleadings. Therefore, unlike in the scenario above where the claimant alleged that she was dismissed because she raised a grievance against her manager for discriminating against her because of her race, which the tribunal accepted as amounting to an allegation of victimisation and resulted in a relabelling exercise i.e. it was an addition to other labels for facts already pleaded to, that cannot be said to be the case here.

---

[139] s.27(1)(a) and s.27(2)(d) Equality Act 2010

Balance the injustice and hardship

5.22　There are an infinite number of scenarios where the balance of injustice and hardship could be considered and lead to an outcome that may be different in a similar case but slightly different circumstances. For example, there may be a case where there is no evidential hardship or injustice on the respondent in that the witnesses needed to defend the case without an amendment are the same witnesses that will be needed to defend the case with the amendment. It might also be that in a case of direct discrimination because of race there is not too much of a material difference in dealing with an amendment to add harassment related to the claimant's race, especially if the alleged discriminator and harasser are one and the same person. Whereas there may well be hardship and injustice on the claimant if such new claim were to be refused. For example, the direct discrimination because of race may potentially be time barred but the harassment related to race, which is a very strong complaint, is not. If, at trial, the claimant's complaint of direct discrimination was found to be time-barred their case would be disposed of in its entirety. Had the new claim of harassment been allowed it would not have caused the respondent any injustice or hardship in defending it. Whereas, it is clear that by *not* allowing the claimant to add the new claim of harassment this has left them with *no* justice and *no* potential remedy, which on balance has led to an injustice and hardship when compared to the respondent's position. Of course, the direct discrimination may not even have been time-barred but failed because the claimant was found not to have been treated less favourably than their comparator.

Time limits

5.23 A request can be made at any time during the proceedings. However, the sooner it is made the better. Notwithstanding this, if a claimant seeks to add a claim that is within the limitation period,[140] then the new claim will almost certainly be allowed because this part is within time in any case. However, if in doubt, obtain a new ACAS certificate,[141] submit a fresh ET1 with the new claim and apply to the tribunal to have the two cases – original and new clam – conjoined.

---

[140] See 4.4-4.8
[141] See 4.3 and 4.7

~ CHAPTER SIX ~

"Some of them are refused the promotion to more responsible posts to which their qualifications entitle them."

Mr James Callaghan[142]

---

[142] 23 April 1968, House of Commons

EMPLOYMENT TRIBUNAL II

6.1 In the First Edition of this book I recorded from the Official Statistics – Tribunal Statistics Quarterly, January to March 2021, "In January to March 2021, 24% of disposals were ACAS conciliated settlements (the most common outcome this quarter), 18% were withdrawn, 17% were dismissed upon withdrawal, 11% were successful at hearing and 9% were struck out (not at a hearing)."[143] The Official Statistics – Tribunal Statistics Quarterly, July to September 2022 reports that 'single claim receipts' have returned to levels seen prior to the COVID-19 pandemic. The **highest maximum award** in 2021/22 was for **Race Discrimination**, at £228,000.[144]

6.2 The overriding objective of the Employment Tribunal Rules of Procedure is to enable employment tribunals to deal with cases fairly and justly. Dealing with a case fairly and justly includes, so far as practicable— (a) ensuring that the parties are on an equal footing; (b) dealing with cases in ways which are proportionate to the complexity and importance of the issues; (c) avoiding unnecessary formality and seeking

---

[143] Official Statistics – Tribunal Statistics Quarterly, January to March 2021, published 10 June 2021
(https://www.gov.uk/government/statistics/tribunal-statistics-quarterly-january-to-march-2021/tribunal-statistics-quarterly-january-to-march-2021#employment-tribunals)

[144] Official Statistics – Tribunal Statistics Quarterly, July to September 2022, published 8 December 2022
(https://www.gov.uk/government/statistics/tribunal-statistics-quarterly-july-to-september-2022/tribunal-statistics-quarterly-july-to-september-2022#employment-tribunals)

flexibility in the proceedings; (d) avoiding delay, so far as compatible with proper consideration of the issues; and (e) saving expense. An employment tribunal shall seek to give effect to the overriding objective in interpreting, or exercising any power given to it by, the rules.[145]

6.3 Many cases are listed for a preliminary hearing with a judge sitting alone to identify the issues in the case, hear any applications (such as, for example, strike out/deposit orders) and to make case management orders to deal with disclosure, preparation of the trial bundle, exchange of witness statements and to list the case for trial.

List of issues

6.4 Despite the clarity of the Grounds of Complaint and Grounds of Resistance, it is useful to have a list of issues to identify what the tribunal is asked to determine both factually and legally. Ideally, the list should be agreed, leaving the tribunal to endorse or to amend as it sees fit. The following are examples of lists of Issues.

6.5 *List of Issues 1*

1. Did the Respondent subject the Claimant to the treatment of refusing to allow him to attend a day release course

---

[145] r.2 of the ET (Constitution & Rules of Procedure) Regs 2013, Sch. 1. Similar rules apply to the Employment Appeal Tribunal – see r.2A of Employment Appeal Tribunal Rules 1993

2. If so, was the treatment *'less favourable treatment'*? i.e. did the Respondent treat the Claimant, who is white, less favourably than Mr. John YY, who is black, in not materially different circumstances?

3. If so, was this because of the Claimant's colour?

6.6 *List of Issues 2*

1. Did the Respondent apply to the Claimants a provision, criterion or practice (PCP) namely:

    (a) Accountants with fewer than five years continuous employment with the Respondent must switch from the DBS to the DCS?

    (b) Accountants must have at least five years employment with the Respondent to have an option to remain in the DBS?

2. If so, did the Respondent apply, or would have applied, the PCP to persons with whom the Claimants do not share the characteristic (English)?

3. If so, does the PCP put, or it would have put, persons with whom the Claimants share a characteristic (Indian origin) at a particular disadvantage when compared with English accountants?

4. If so, does it put or would it put, the Claimants at that disadvantage?

5. If so, can the Respondent show the PCP to be a proportionate means of achieving a legitimate aim?

6.7 *List of Issues 3*

1. Did the Respondent (Mr. Phil TT) engage in racial remarks such as, "XXX," "YYY," and "ZZZ," at the Respondent's function on 13 December 2019?

2. If so, was that conduct unwanted? The Claimant says she told Mr. Phil TT to stop his conduct as she found his comments quite offensive, but he continued with making similar remarks. Also, the Claimant says on 16 December 2019 she complained to her supervisor, Ms. Sylvia WW, about her being harassed by Mr. Phil TT to which Ms. Sylvia WW said that he probably had too much to drink, and that the Claimant should, "loosen up a little."

3. If so, did it relate to the protected characteristic of race?

4. If so, did the conduct have the purpose or effect of violating the Claimant's dignity or creating an intimidating, hostile, degrading, humiliating or offensive environment for her?

5. If so, did the Respondent take all reasonable steps to prevent Mr. Phil TT from making racist remarks and

or harassing others in the course of his employment or from doing anything of that description?

6.8 *List of Issues 4*

1. Did the Claimant do a protected act? The Claimant relies on her grievance raised against her manager, Mr. Stan PP, in which she says she alleged that he had discriminated against her because of her race. The Respondent denies that she alleged race discrimination in her grievance and thus denies she make a protected act.

2. If the Claimant did do a protected act, did the Respondent dismiss her because she did the protected act?

Strike out/deposit orders

6.9 Sometimes a party would make an application to have the opponent's claim/response struck out because it is of the view that their claim/response has no reasonable prospect of success or the tribunal makes a deposit order, not exceeding £1000 as a condition of continuing to advance that allegation or argument, because the claim/response has little reasonable prospect of success. However, before making such an order the tribunal must make reasonable enquiries into the paying party's ability to pay the deposit and have regard to any such information when deciding the amount of the deposit. The tribunal's reasons for making the deposit order must be provided with the order and the paying party would be notified of the potential consequences of the order. However, if the party against whom the deposit order is made fails to pay the deposit by the due date the specific allegation or argument to which the deposit order relates shall be struck out.[146] In its Grounds of Resistance in response to Claim 4 (Stephanie v ABCD Pubs Ltd) the Respondent put the Claimant on notice of its application to follow due to its contention that the grievance did not amount to a protected act and, therefore, the Claimant could not succeed in her claim of victimisation.

Tribunal Orders

6.10 There are an infinite number of orders a tribunal can make, which would be dependent on the circumstances of the case. I shall deal with the main ones that apply to all cases.

Disclosure

6.11 A useful tool for claimants, which is *not* part of the tribunal process and procedure, is the use of a subject access request from their employers (SAR). "You have the right to ask an organisation whether or not they are using or storing your personal information. You can also ask them for copies of your personal information, verbally or in writing."[147] You should receive a response to a SAR within one month.

---

[146] r.39 of the ET (Constitution & Rules of Procedure) Regs 2013, Sch. 1
[147] Information Commissioner's Office (ico.) https://ico.org.uk/your-data-matters/your-right-to-get-copies-of-your-data/

However, this can be extended by an additional two months if, 'you have made a number of requests or your request is complex." If the additional two months are required, the employer should let the employee know within one month, stating their reasons. Note that employers occasionally charge a fee for the costs of providing the documents requested and may, "charge a reasonable fee to cover their administrative costs – if they think your request is 'manifestly unfounded or excessive.'"[148] A SAR often leads to a claimant obtaining supporting information for their case that, but for their SAR, may not necessarily have been disclosed as part of the ordinary tribunal disclosure procedure.

6.12 The parties must send each other copies of all the documents they have relevant to the claim, including those relevant to financial losses. If, as in the case of Stephanie in Claim 4, the claimant was dismissed, they will have to show that they sought to mitigate those losses by showing what they have done to secure alternative employment. The Respondent, on the other hand, might, if it believes this to be the case, wish to provide documents to show why the claimant has failed to mitigate her losses because, for example, there were/are vacancies she could have filled or jobs she could have applied for. Such disclosure will include, amongst other things, recordings, emails, text messages, social media and other electronic information. Parties must

---

[148] Information Commissioner's Office (ico.) https://ico.org.uk/your-data-matters/your-right-to-get-copies-of-your-data/what-to-expect-after-making-a-subject-access-request/

send all relevant documents they have in their possession or control even if they do not support their case. The parties would then agree which documents are going to be used at the hearing.

Bundle

6.13 It is common for the company respondent to prepare the trial bundle, but the parties can agree on another party having this responsibility and send the bundle to the other party/parties. The bundle must have an index, page numbers and arranged as far as possible in a chronological order.

Witness statements

6.14 In England and Wales, the parties will provide their evidence by way of witness statements that must contain all their evidence on which they wish to rely at trial. This evidence is what is termed, 'evidence-in-chief.' In Scotland, witness statements are an option. A witness statement will normally take a similar form as below. However, when the evidence is presented, the burden of proof is *ultimately* on the claimant to prove their case. But discrimination cases are unique, to some degree, in the sense that alleged discriminatory acts are more covert than overt. So, if there are facts from which the tribunal could decide, in the absence of any other explanation, that the respondent has, for example, discriminated against, harassed or victimised the claimant, the tribunal must hold that the contravention occurred. "The inference cannot be drawn from the fact that other employers sometimes discriminate in such circumstances; it cannot be inferred that A discriminates merely because B, C and D have been known to do so in similar circumstances. That is a plainly deficient basis for inferring discrimination. It would be wholly unjust to make a finding of such serious import on such a flawed basis."[149]

6.14.1 As recently confirmed by the UK Supreme Court, "The central point made in [s.136(2) of the Equality Act 2010 that, 'If there are facts from which the court could decide, in the absence of any other explanation, that a person (A) contravened the provision concerned, the court must hold that the contravention occurred,'] requires the employment tribunal to consider all the evidence from all sources, not just the claimant's evidence, so as to decide whether or not "there are facts etc"."[150] Therefore, the employer would not be liable if they are able to show that they did not contravene the 2010 Act as alleged. "…one of the reasons for the (partial) reversal of the burden of proof which it effects is that it can often be very difficult for a claimant to prove what is going on in the mind of the putative discriminator. I believe that the Tribunal had this very much in mind."[151] It is important to bear in mind, however, the burden of proof is still on the claimant at the first stage of

---

[149] *The Law Society and others (appellants) v. Bahl (respondent) [2003] IRLR 640*
[150] *Royal Mail Group Ltd (Respondent) v Efobi (Appellant) [2021] UKSC 33*
[151] *Base Childrenswear Ltd (appellant) v Otshudi (respondent) [2020] IRLR 118; [2019] EWCA Civ 1648*

the enquiry in discrimination cases and that had not been removed by s.136 of the Equality Act 2010.[152]

6.15 *Claimant*

Case No. 12345/2020

IN THE ABCDEFG EMPLOYMENT TRIBUNALS

BETWEEN:

Mr. Delroy HH

<u>Claimant</u>

-and-

A. Chartered Surveyors in Bristol

<u>Respondent</u>

<u>**WITNESS STATEMENT OF DELROY JAMES HH**</u>

I, Delroy James HH, of 123 Somewhere Street, Someplace, S?? ??2 will say as follows:

1. I am the Claimant in this matter and make this statement in support of my claim of race discrimination against the Respondent.

2. I am white and have been employed by the Respondent has a junior surveyor since 7 January 2019. My contract of employment is at page X.

---

[152] *Ayodele (appellant) v Citylink Ltd and another (respondents) [2018] IRLR 114; [2018] ICR 748; [2017] EWCA Civ 1913*

3. The Respondent is a firm of Chartered Surveyors, employing 15 surveyors. From the 15 surveyors five were ranked as junior, of which I was one. The juniors undertake all aspects of surveying expected of their rank such as, but not limited to, XYZ. My job description (JD) is at page XX.

4. The main distinction between senior and junior surveyors is that the former are Chartered and the latter are not. In order to become Chartered it is common for a junior to begin the academic stage of their studies by undertaking, for example, a BSc in Surveying.

5. In or around January 2021 I asked Marsha LL, a partner of the Respondent, whether I could attend a day release course and was refused on the basis that the covid pandemic had meant that the Respondent had made a loss and there was now a freeze on the training budget. I was very disappointed but understood. I remember thinking that I wish I had waited until Ms. Julia MM, the practice manager, returned from her holiday and asked her instead. However, when she returned from holiday I decided not to mention it.

6. On or around 1 March 2021 Mr. John YY, who is black, joined the Respondent as a junior surveyor and undertook the same surveying duties as all the juniors. To my surprise, in April 2021 I discovered that Mr.

John YY was allowed to attend a day release degree course. John and I are good friends and I am glad that the Respondent has given him this opportunity, but so should I have had the same opportunity.

7. I dispute the Respondent's explanation about a freeze on the training budget because Mr. John YY would still be out of the office at least one day a week and probably allowed extra time off for exams etc. This opportunity was not offered to me.

8. I believe that by not allowing me to study one day a week, as it did for Mr. John YY, the Respondent treated me less favourably than him and thus directly discriminated against me because of my race.

9. The contents of this statement are true to my best belief and knowledge.

NAME……………………………………………..

SIGNED……………………………………………

DATED……………………………………………..

6.16　*Respondent*

[HEADING SAME AS THE CLAIMANT]

WITNESS STATEMENT OF MARSHA LYRA LL

I, Marsha Lyra LL, of 123 Somewhereelse Road, Bristol, B?? ??2 will say as follows:

1. I am a partner of the Respondent and worked for the Respondent for 14 years before I was made a partner 7 years ago. I make this statement in support of the Respondent. The facts stated are from my personal experience. Where they do not come from my personal experience, I have a reasonable belief that they are true.

2. We strenuously deny racially discriminating against the Claimant. We are an equal opportunities employer. All our staff and partners attend diversity awareness & inclusion and equal opportunities courses regularly and, in any case, bi-annually (every two years).

3. Without giving too much financially sensitive information, due to the covid pandemic the Respondent had made a significant financial loss and rather than reduce our headcount we sought to reduce our costs. Training was identified as an area we could reduce costs temporarily and decided to impose a freeze on the training budget for those not already attending courses. Therefore, when the Claimant spoke to me about attending a day release course, I explained to him the position. He seemed to understand, and that was the last I heard about his desire.

4. In or around November 2020 we had the first of two interviews with Mr. John YY. He came from another firm of Chartered Surveyors and had been due to commence his degree in September 2020 but that was postponed to September 2021. His previous firm had paid for the course in July 2020 and waived the right for John YY to refund them the fees when he left, as it was not his fault that the course was postponed in September 2020. I think they were happy that he had found a job because they announced that some of their surveyors were at risk of redundancy.

5. I am pleased to say that on 1 February 2021 Mr. John YY accepted our offer to join us as a junior surveyor. We saw it as a no brainer for John to attend a course that had already been paid for. The least we could give him was the time off one day a week to attend his course. From our experience, even though we don't encourage it, we witness no significant shortfall in output from our junior surveyors attending college/university one day a week and definitely not a 20% reduction. So, this was an easy investment for us. We hope that by 2022 we would be in a position to lift the training freeze. Had the Claimant spoken to us about his concerns we could have enlightened him. But he chose to make this spurious claim about race discrimination about which I am personally very deeply offended.

6. To be clear, we did not treat the Claimant less favourably than John because their circumstances were entirely different for reasons I have already given and definitely did not discriminate against him at all, let alone because of his colour. In fact, the Claimant claims he was discriminated against on 1 January 2021, but John wasn't even an employee of ours.

7. The contents of this statement are true to my best belief and knowledge.

NAME………………………………………….

SIGNED………………………………………….

DATED………………………………………….

Mediation

6.17 "A Tribunal shall wherever practicable and appropriate encourage the use by the parties of the services of ACAS, judicial or other mediation, or other means of resolving their disputes by agreement."[153] There are two main types of mediation when it comes to employment. An internal dispute can be resolved internally or in the case of employment tribunal parties can opt for judicial mediation.

---

[153] r3 of the ET (Constitution & Rules of Procedure) Regs 2013, Sch. 1

In the workplace

6.18 Mediation in the workplace has the advantage of being resolved locally before it escalates to a grievance or externally to an employment tribunal. It would also save on, potentially, costs for lawyers; time preparing for trial; and the inevitable pressures of dealing with litigation, which should not be underestimated. The mediator would be an employee trained in mediation that has been accredited by one of many external providers. If no such person exists within the company or, for other reasons the person is unable to conduct the mediation – for example, the person is a party to the dispute in question – a company, if it so wishes, may well instruct an external mediator. Notably, "The mediator is not there to judge, to say one person is right and the other wrong, or to tell those involved in the mediation what they should do."[154]

Employment Tribunal Service – Judicial Mediation

6.19 Where a case has gone to the employment tribunal, the parties can opt to attend judicial mediation. The mediator would be an employment judge trained to be and acting as a mediator on the day. Parties could be represented at a judicial mediation. Mediations are a useful way of resolving disputes. They also avoid adversary in which litigation is likely to result. Judicial mediation can occur at any time during proceedings but, from experience, the best time is sooner rather than later for two main reasons. Firstly,

---

[154] The Guide, p9

significant costs are yet to be incurred by the parties. Secondly, *before* witness statements have been exchanged because what parties say in support of their cases and against their opponent can act as a barrier to reasoning and resolving an issue.

6.20 Parties should keep in mind that their participation is voluntary. That means they can walk away at any time during the process. However, once they have decided to enter this process, they should at least give it their best try and expect that both sides are likely to compromise to some degree. If a matter is resolved through judicial mediation, the parties can decide how to document their agreement. A common way would be to involve ACAS and enter into a COT3. Upon agreement that would be the end of the judicial mediation and, in turn, the employment tribunal proceedings. The claim would be dismissed by the employment tribunal upon the claimant's withdrawal, which is likely to have been a term under the COT3 or other agreement.

Settlement Agreement/Without prejudice offer/COT3

6.21 At any stage during the proceedings the parties can enter into 'without prejudice' discussions to settle their dispute. Normally, this would entail the Respondent offering the Claimant a sum of money, usually without any admission of liability. Or, the Claimant may simply wish to withdraw their case for a variety of reasons, one of which could be to avoid the risk of costs due to their case being weak or weaker than when they issued their claim. If parties reach an agreement as a result of their without prejudice discussion, there are primarily two agreements they can choose from. One is a COT3 and the other is a settlement agreement.

COT 3

6.22 This form is normally simple in mode and contains only a few paragraphs. There will be a live dispute in the employment tribunal and involve ACAS. The COT3 is binding on the parties the moment it is agreed orally, upon which the employment tribunal will be contacted and informed accordingly to dismiss the claim upon withdrawal. The parties can agree whatever they so wish, but below is an example of a basic COT3.

<u>COT 3</u>

1. The Respondent agrees not to pursue the Claimant for the costs incurred by it in defending the Employment Tribunal claims under case number 12345/2020 (the Claim) brought by the Claimant in consideration for the Claimant withdrawing the Claim.

2. This settlement shall not affect any accrued pension rights that the Claimant may have, nor any claim for personal injury about which the Claimant is currently unaware and could not reasonably be aware at the date of this Agreement, nor the right to make a disclosure of information in compliance with the strict

provisions of the Employment Rights Act 1996 (whistleblowing). By entering into this Agreement, the Claimant confirms that he is unaware of any circumstances that would give rise to any personal injury claim and that there is no such claim pending at the date of this Agreement.

3. The Claimant will:

   (a) write to the Employment Tribunal to withdraw the Claim (Withdrawal Letter) within 5 business days of the oral agreement of this Agreement through ACAS; and

   (b) send a copy of the Withdrawal Letter to the Respondent on the same day that it is sent to the Employment Tribunal.

4. The Parties acknowledge that, following withdrawal of the Claim by the Claimant, the proceedings covered by this settlement will be dismissed by the Employment Tribunal.

5. If the Claimant subsequently issues or pursues any proceedings in breach of this Agreement, then the Respondent will pursue the Claimant for the costs and expenses incurred by it in defending the Claim.

6. The Claimant and Respondent shall keep the existence and terms of this settlement confidential except where disclosure is required by law or to their legal or

professional advisers or immediate family (provided that they agree to keep the information confidential).

**Signed by or on behalf of
Delroy James HH**

....
Date..................

**Signed for and on behalf of
A. Chartered Surveyors in Bristol**

....
Date..................

6.22.1 In a recent case,[155] the claimant was employed by the respondent between May 2014 and June 2014, following which he presented a complaint of race discrimination against the respondent in the same year. In January 2018 he applied for a post with a wholly owned subsidiary of the respondent, which was rejected in February 2018. In March 2018 the parties settled the 2014 complaint by way of a COT3. It was a term of the settlement that, 'The claimant agrees that the payment set out in paragraph 1 is accepted in full and final settlement of all or any costs, claims, expenses or rights of action of any kind

---

[155] *Arvunescu (appellant) v Quick Release (Automotive) Ltd (respondent)* [2023] IRLR 230; 2023] ICR 271; [2022] EWCA Civ 1600

whatsoever, wheresoever and howsoever arising under common law, statute or otherwise (whether or not within the jurisdiction of the employment tribunal) which the claimant has or may have against the respondent or against any employee, agent or officer of the respondent arising directly or indirectly out of or in connection with the claimant's employment with the respondent, its termination or otherwise. This paragraph applies to a claim even though the claimant may be unaware at the date of this agreement of the circumstances which might give rise to it or the legal basis for such a claim.'

6.22.2 In May 2018 the claimant brought a claim of victimisation against the respondent, alleging that he had been victimised in February 2018 by being rejected for the post with its wholly owned subsidiary. He alleged that due to its close links with the subsidiary it had been responsible for the said rejection. The question to be determined, which went to the Court of Appeal, was whether the COT3 (March 2018) prevented the claimant from bringing the claim and having it heard; after all, at the time he applied for the post (January 2018) he was not an employee of the respondent (employment ended in June 2014) so how can he be said to settle an issue occurring in February 2018 (rejection) in a COT3 dealing with a claim made in March 2014?

6.22.3 It was held that the May 2018 claim fell within the wording of the March 2018 COT3 agreement. Although it did not arise directly or indirectly out of the claimant's employment with the respondent, the COT3 was nevertheless expressed more widely than that. By including that claims arising 'indirectly ... in connection with the employment,' the May 2018 claim did arise indirectly in connection with the employment. It should be noted that, although the claimant was not an employee in March 2018 (COT3), as the rejection was in February 2018 and, thus, prior to the date of his entering into the COT3 – in other words he knew of the rejection *prior to* entering into the COT3 – in March 2018, he was bound by the terms *as from that date*. For completion, the May 2018 date (claim lodged) is irrelevant to the issue because no claim arose at that time, the complaint was simply presented to the employment tribunal at that time.

6.22.4 Contrast the above case with a case that involved a post-termination claim, following a settlement agreement, which I discuss below.[156]

Settlement Agreement

6.23 There does not need to be a live action before the Employment Tribunal for the employer and employee to enter into a settlement agreement. For example, they may agree mutually to terminate the contract of employment on the basis that the employer pays an agreed sum of money and in return the employee agreeing to waive their rights to bring a claim against the employer for terminating the

---

[156] *Bathgate (appellant) v Technip UK Ltd and others (respondents)* [2022] EAT 155; [2023] IRLR 4

contract or matters arising from the employment. This type of settlement tends to be longer, running into many pages, and more detailed than a COT3. Whereas a COT3 necessarily involves ACAS and is binding on the parties upon their verbal agreement of the terms, a settlement agreement is binding on the parties upon the signing of the agreement. Furthermore, to be a qualifying settlement agreement, for our purposes[157], there are various conditions to be met, which shall not be repeated fully here but the reader is referred to s.147 of the Equality Act 2010 extract recited in Chapter Ten. Some of the conditions are that—(a) the contract is in writing, (b) the contract relates to the particular complaint, (c) the complainant has, before entering into the contract, received advice from an independent adviser about its terms and effect (including, in particular, its effect on the complainant's ability to pursue the complaint before an employment tribunal), (d) on the date of the giving of the advice, there is in force a contract of insurance, or an indemnity provided for members of a profession or professional body, covering the risk of a claim by the complainant in respect of loss arising from the advice, (e) the contract identifies the adviser, and (f) the contract states that the conditions in paragraphs (c) and (d) are met. Each of the following is an independent adviser— (a) a qualified lawyer; (b) an officer, official, employee or member of an independent trade union certified in writing by the trade union as competent to give advice and as authorised to do so on its behalf; (c) a worker at an advice

---

[157] Other statutes have similar wording, which is relevant to the type of complaints being settled.

centre (whether as an employee or a volunteer) certified in writing by the centre as competent to give advice and as authorised to do so on its behalf; and (d) a person of such description as may be specified by order.

6.24 Naturally, a settlement agreement may take various forms and, therefore, a full example is beyond the scope of this book. However, an example of an opening may be as follows.

6.25

Settlement Agreement

This agreement is dated [   ] August 2021.

Parties

(1) The ABCXYZ??? Limited incorporated and registered in England and Wales with company number 12345678910 whose registered office is at Anywhere House, Any Where Street, Anywhere, AN? ?WH (**Company**)

(2) Mr. G. Employee of Worker Road, ?? Worker, WO? ?ER (**Employee**)

BACKGROUND

(A) You were employed by us from 1 January 2015 as Operations Manager under a contract dated 1 January 2015.

(B) Your employment with the Company shall terminate on 30 September 2021.

(C) The parties have entered into this agreement to record and implement the terms on which they have agreed to settle any claims that you have or may have in connection with your employment or its termination or otherwise against the Company, its officers, employees or workers, whether or not those claims are, or could be, in the contemplation of the parties at the time of signing this agreement, and including, in particular, the statutory complaints that you raise in this agreement.

(D) The parties intend this agreement to be an effective waiver of any such claims and to satisfy the conditions relating to settlement agreements in the relevant legislation.

Agreed terms

1. Interpretation

The following definitions and rules of interpretation apply in this agreement.

1.1 Definitions:

Adviser: ABC DEFG of Lawyers .

2. Arrangements on termination

2.1 Your employment with the Company shall terminate on 30 September 2021 (**Termination Date**).

2.2 The Company shall pay you your salary up to the Termination Date in the usual way.

2.3 At the Termination Date, you will have no outstanding accrued holiday.

2.4 On 30 September 2021 the Company shall make a payment to you in lieu of your notice entitlement in the amount of £???? (the PILON)…

2.5 The payments and benefits are all made subject to the income tax and National Insurance contributions that we are obliged by law to pay or deduct.

3. **Termination payment**

3.1 Subject to and conditional on you complying with the terms of this agreement, the Company shall within 21 days of the Termination Date or receipt by us of a copy of this agreement signed by you and a letter from the Adviser…Pay you the sum of £… (**Termination Payment**).

3.2 The Company will pay the Termination Payment less all required deductions for tax and National Insurance contributions.

3.3 You shall be responsible for any further tax and employee's National Insurance contributions due in respect of the Termination Payment and shall indemnify us in respect of such liability in accordance with…

4. **Waiver of claims**

4.1 You agree that the terms of this agreement are offered by the Company without any admission of liability on its part and are in full and final settlement of all and any claims or rights of action that you have or may have against the Company or its officers, employees or workers arising out of your employment with us or its termination, whether under common law, contract, statute or otherwise, whether such claims are, or could be, known to the parties or in their contemplation at the date of this agreement in any jurisdiction and including, but not limited to, the claims specified in… (each of which is waived by this clause).

4.2 You warrant that:

(a) before entering into this agreement you received independent advice from the Adviser as to the terms and effect of this agreement and, in particular, on its effect on your ability to pursue the claims specified in… to this agreement;

(b) the Adviser has confirmed to you that they are a barrister holding a current practising certificate and that there is in force a policy of insurance covering the risk of a claim by you in respect of any loss arising in consequence of their advice;

(c) the Adviser shall sign and deliver to us a letter in the form attached as… to this agreement;

(d) before receiving the advice you disclosed to the Adviser all facts and circumstances that may give rise to a claim by you against the Company or its officers, employees or workers;

(e) the only claims that you have or may have against the Company or its officers, employees or workers (whether at the time of entering into this agreement or in the future) relating to your employment with us or its termination are specified in…; and

(f) You are not aware of any facts or circumstances that may give rise to any claim against the Company or its officers, employees or workers other than those claims specified in…

You acknowledge that the Company acted in reliance on these warranties when entering into this agreement.

4.3 You acknowledge that the conditions relating to settlement agreements under section 147(3) of the Equality Act 2010… have been satisfied.

4.4 The waiver in… shall have effect irrespective of whether or not, at the date of this agreement, you are or could be aware of such claims or have such claims in your express contemplation (including such claims of which you become aware after the date of this agreement in whole or in part as a result of new legislation or the development of common law or equity).

5. Tribunal proceedings

5.1 Immediately on execution of this agreement, you shall notify the employment tribunal in writing that the claim against the Company in case number …./2020 (which includes, but not is not limited to, claims for discrimination because of race is withdrawn irrevocably having been settled by this agreement, and should be dismissed). You shall immediately send a copy of such notification to our lawyers…

5.2 Neither party shall make or pursue any application for costs, preparation time or wasted costs in connection with that claim.

6. Governing law

This agreement and any dispute or claim arising out of or in connection with it or its subject matter or formation (including non-contractual disputes or claims) shall be governed by and construed in accordance with the law of England and Wales.

7. **Jurisdiction**

   Each party irrevocably agrees that the courts of England and Wales shall have exclusive jurisdiction to settle any dispute or claim arising out of or in connection with this agreement or its subject matter or formation (including non-contractual disputes or claims).

8. **Subject to contract and without prejudice**

   This agreement shall be deemed to be without prejudice and subject to contract until such time as it is signed by both parties and dated, when it shall be treated as an open document evidencing a binding agreement.

   This agreement has been entered into on the date stated at the beginning of it.

6.25.1 In a recent case,[158] the claimant entered into a voluntary redundancy agreement by way of a settlement agreement in January 2017. It with a term of the settlement agreement that, '… the Employee's particular complaints and claims which, however unjustified they may be regarded by the Company, the Employee hereby intimates and asserts against the Company while at the same time acknowledging that they are not to be pursued further, namely, claims ("Claims"): … (j) for direct or indirect discrimination, harassment or victimisation related to: … (v) age, under

---

[158] *Bathgate (appellant) v Technip UK Ltd and others (respondents)* [2022] EAT 155; [2023] IRLR 4

section 120 of the Equality Act 2010 and/or regulation 36 of the Employment Equality (Age) Regulations 2006.'

6.25.2 In addition to other payments, the claimant, who was aged 61, was under the impression that under the terms of the settlement agreement an enhanced payment would be due and payable to him in June 2017. However, the respondent was under the impression that it did not need to pay employees who were aged 61 and over in the circumstances. The claimant presented a complaint of direct and indirect age discrimination against the respondent. The question before the EAT was, did the terms of the settlement agreement, reached in January 2017, prevent him from presenting the complaints of discrimination that arose from the failure to pay June 2017?

6.25.3 The EAT held that under s.147 of the Equality Act 2010 settlement agreements cannot prohibit future potential complaints. The EAT said, "The words 'the particular complaint' suggest that Parliament anticipated the existence of an actual complaint or circumstances where the grounds for a complaint existed. I do not consider that the words 'the particular complaint' are apt to describe a potential future complaint."[159] In other words, unlike with the case we discussed at 6.22.1-3, the claimant could not have settled in January 2017 a non-payment 5 months in June 2017 as he could not *possibly* have known this would happen. Furthermore, the alleged breach of June 2017 did not *itself* occur/*was not* in existence at the time of entering into the

---

[159] Para. 25

settlement agreement (January 2017), whereas in the COT3 case the rejection occurred before the parties entered into the COT3. In consequence, for example, it is difficult to see how a respondent could argue *successfully* that a claimant settled a complaint based on a *post-settlement* reference provided by the respondent to which the claimant takes offence and on which basis, therefore, the claimant wishes to present a complaint to the employment tribunal.

Without prejudice save as to costs

6.26 The COT3 and Settlement Agreement are based on a successful conclusion of negotiations between the parties. However, not all negotiations conclude or end successfully, and not all offers are accepted. At the commencement of any discussion to seek to settle a matter, parties will normally agree that such will take place on a 'without prejudice' basis. This means that the discussions are protected from being published or shared outside the parties involved. If offers are accepted then all well and good. If they are not, a paying party or the party that suggest a 'drop hands' approach (both parties walk away and bear their own legal costs), are likely to append the words, 'save as to costs,' to read, 'without prejudice save as to costs.' This means that discussions remain protected from being published or shared outside those immediately involved, but now the issue of costs is not protected and discussions and documents *can* be published at the appropriate time if need be. If a party was offered, say, £10,000 on 1 January 2021 on a 'without prejudice save as to costs' basis to settle a case and rejects that offer, opting to take their chances at court. If they fail to beat that offer at court due to their losing or winning, but are awarded a lower compensation, say £5,000, the other party will *then* bring to the tribunal's attention the 'without prejudice save as to costs,' offer made on 1 January 2021. They would argue that it was unreasonable for the claimant to have continued with their case beyond 1 January 2021 because they had offered more to the claimant than the claimant was awarded by the tribunal. On this basis, the other party would have a strong case for the recovery of its costs from that date onwards. Note, it is highly unlikely that, in the absence of a costs warning letter made prior to 1 January 2021, an award would be made for costs incurred before 1 January 2021.

The Hearing

6.27 Discrimination cases are normally heard by a fully constituted tribunal, being a panel of three, consisting of an employment judge (lawyer) and two lay people (non-lawyers, often termed 'wing members' because they tend to sit one either side of the employment judge). In the old days, the witness used to read their statements aloud in open court, which was somewhat frustrating for some because, naturally, many of those involved in the preparation of the case had already read them. Today, the tribunal arrange to have 'reading time' ahead of cross examination and proceed on the basis as if the witness had said orally in open court what is written in their signed statement. To ensure that what is written is what the witness wishes to say, they are sworn in (either swear on a holy book or take the oath to tell the truth) and confirm that the contents, with any amendments they wish to make, are the evidence they rely on. Some tribunals grant leave (allow) for supplementary questions where some clarity may be needed from the outset before cross examinations. Any supplementary questions ought rightly to be open-ended questions because questions dealing with evidence-in-chief should not be leading (i.e. putting/framing a question in such a way as to get or guarantee the answer you desire). Open-ended questions are those that start with, "how, what, why, when etc?" or commands such as "describe, explain, tell me about etc."

6.28 After a witness is sworn in and adopt their statement as their evidence, they are cross examined. The art of cross examination is beyond the scope of this book, but the following may be helpful. In cross examination the opposing party is there to challenge parts of the witness' evidence and to put the opposing party's case to the relevant witness. I say the relevant witness because it would be fruitless to put a question to a witness who could either not answer a question because they were not involved in what is being put to them or another witness would be better placed to answer that line of questioning. It is important that the questioner prepares thoroughly. One can *never* be over prepared. The order in which one puts their questions is important. The same set of questions used in the wrong order can have a different impact or, dare I say, a different result. For example, you would not want to start with:

6.29 "Why did you discriminate against me because of my race?"

No guessing what the response will be beyond, "I didn't discriminate against you at all." It also allows the witness to tell *and* elaborate on *their* case when you are supposed to be putting *your* case to *them*. You don't want an opposing witness to gate-crash your party! So, one way to avoid this is to use as many close-ended questions as possible – those with 'yes' or 'no' answers. If the witness needs to elaborate on an answer because 'yes' or 'no' does not give the full picture, they may be allowed to elaborate a little or they can deal with that in re-examination, which I shall touch on below. So, our opening question might be better put and more effective as:

6.30 "In January 2021, I asked you to attend a day release course, didn't I?"
"Yes."
"You said no, didn't you?"
"Yes!"
"You said no because, "the Respondent had made a loss and there was now a freeze on the training budget." That's what you said, you didn't you?"
"Yes."
"You permitted Mr. John YY to attend a day release course, didn't you?"
"Yes."

"It is a BSc day release course in surveying, isn't it?"

"Yes."

"Do you accept that the course he will be attending is similar to, if not the same as, the course that I asked you to attend?"

"Yes."

"The reason you refused my request to do the very same course as Mr. John YY is because of my colour, isn't it?"

"No."

6.31 The answers are unlikely to be as straightforward as the above because there will be occasions when the witness will want to add more. However, the skill is to anticipate this and to think of supplementary question if an answer is different to what you would want or a brief elaboration sheds a different light to the 'yes' or 'no' answer. For example:

6.32 "Do you accept that the course he will be attending is the same course that I asked you to attend?"

"Yes, but we were not going to pay for the course."

"Did you inquire into how much the course would cost?"

"No because there was no budget for training. There was no point."

"However, having permitted Mr. John YY to attend college, did you not see it as incumbent on you to at least inquire to see whether we could both attend because you would have two students training for the price of one, effectively?"

"No."

6.33 Now, you have painted a picture that allows you to make a submission on how seriously (or not) the employer views 'equality of opportunity.' This also covers that at the time the less favourable treatment was alleged to have occurred (January 2021) John, the named comparator, was not even employed by the Respondent. In this case 'equality of opportunity to attend the day release course.' It will not necessarily be as easy as this, but the point is to think in advance where the line of questioning could go rather than simply where, ideally, you would want it to go.

6.34 Occasionally, the tribunal will seek clarification as the witness gives evidence (being cross examined). Many, however, will wait for when cross-examination has been concluded and raise their questions. It is important to note that the tribunal is not allowed to cross-examine a witness. However, notwithstanding that, a witness would treat their questions lightly at their peril! After their questions, the witness will be re-examined by their own representative or, if representing themselves, the employment judge will ask whether there is anything they wish to say that arose from the cross examination and the tribunal's questioning. For example:

6.35 "You were asked, 'did you not see it as incumbent on you at least to inquire to see whether both the Claimant and Mr. John YY could attend because you would have two students training for the price of one.' Can you explain how permitting Mr. John YY to attend a course one day a week impacts the freeze on the training budget."

"It doesn't impact on it at all because we are not paying for it."

"Can you explain how permitting the Claimant to attend a course one day a week impacts the freeze on the training budget."

"It would because there is a freeze and we would be liable for the course fees, which could only come from the training budget."

"When you were asked whether you saw it as incumbent on you to at least inquire to see if both could attend the course, you replied no. Why did you say that?"

"Because the freeze was on the training budget. Allowing Mr. John YY had no impact on that decision. Permitting both would mean that I would have been committing us to an expense for which I had no permission. I would simply be increasing our losses. The idea was to keep the practice solvent in difficult times, to avoid seeking to reduce salaries or, worst, make redundancies. We decided that as we had lost two surveyors in December, John's appointment was an opportunity we could not let pass us by."

6.36 The order of evidence-in-chief, cross examination, tribunal questions and re-examination are repeated for each witness. They are followed by closing submissions. This is where the parties sum-up their case, referring to the evidence and seek to convince the tribunal why they should succeed in their claim or response/defence. Such closings can be done solely orally, solely in writing or a mixture of the two. No one method or form carries more weight over the other(s). It is not uncommon, however, for the tribunal to seek clarification on submissions.

6.37 After submissions, the tribunal will decide whether to deliberate (consider the evidence and submissions) immediately and give an oral judgment in open court within the time listed or reserve judgment and send it out in written form to the parties with full written reasons, 'as soon as practicable.'[160] If the tribunal decides to deliberate immediately, it will inform the parties when judgment is likely to be given. For example, it might advise the parties to return in the afternoon or the next day etc. Either way, judgment is given in open court and is given by the employment judge (the person in the middle) who informs the parties whether the decision/judgment was reached by a unanimous or majority vote. Judges have different styles on how they deliver their judgments, but the contents are the same in that the parties will be informed primarily, with reference to the findings of fact and the law, why they won or lost along with their reasons. Where reasons were given orally, the Employment Judge will announce that written reasons will not be provided unless they are asked for by any party at the hearing itself or by a written request presented by any party within 14 days of the sending of the written record of the decision.[161]

---

[160] r.61(1) of the ET (Constitution & Rules of Procedure) Regs 2013, Sch. 1
[161] r.62(3) of the ET (Constitution & Rules of Procedure) Regs 2013, Sch. 1

Remedy

6.38 If the claimant wins their case, the employment tribunal will hold a remedy hearing for which the claimant would often have prepared an updated schedule of loss. As can be seen from the Grounds of Complaints in claims 1 to 3 above, the tribunal may—(a) make a declaration as to the rights of the complainant and the respondent in relation to the matters to which the proceedings relate. A claimant would normally request that the tribunal declare that they have been unlawfully discriminated against, harassed and or victimised. If the claimant is still employed, they may ask the employment tribunal to make a recommendation. "An appropriate recommendation is a recommendation that within a specified period the respondent takes specified steps for the purpose of obviating or reducing the adverse effect on the complainant of any matter to which the proceedings relate."[162] It is common for the claimant to ask that the tribunal recommend that the employer undertake equal opportunities training. Finally, is the issue of compensation. The last is probably the main remedy sought by claimants. In a case where dismissal is found to be an act of unlawful discrimination the claimant must demonstrate that they have attempted to mitigate their loses, which will be taken into account when considering how much is 'fair etc' to award. Whether or not a claimant has suffered a financial loss, they will be eligible for an award for injury to feelings.[163]

---

[162] s124(3) of the Equality Act 2010
[163] s119(4) and s124(6) of the Equality Act 2010

6.39 In an EAT case,[164] the principles drawn from various authorities were summarised as follows:

(1) Awards for injury to feelings are compensatory. They should be just to both parties. They should compensate fully without punishing the tortfeasor. Feelings of indignation at the tortfeasor's conduct should not be allowed to inflate the award.

(2) Awards should not be too low, as that would diminish respect for the policy of the anti-discrimination legislation. Society has condemned discrimination and awards must ensure that it is seen to be wrong. On the other hand, awards should be restrained, as excessive awards could, to use Lord Bingham's phrase, be seen as the way to untaxed riches.

(3) Awards should bear some broad general similarity to the range of awards in personal injury cases. We do not think this should be done by reference to any particular type of personal injury award; rather to the whole range of such awards.

(4) In exercising their discretion in assessing a sum, tribunals should remind themselves of the value in everyday life of the sum they have in mind. This may be done by reference to purchasing power or by reference to earnings.

---

[164] *(1) Armitage, (2) Marsden and (3) H M Prison Service (appellants) v. Johnson (respondent) [1997] IRLR 162*

(5) Finally, tribunals should bear in mind Lord Bingham's reference to the need for public respect for the level of awards made.

6.40 On rare occasions aggravated damages may be awarded in addition to the general compensatory award (for losses and injury to feelings) if the following is satisfied:

(1) Aggravated damages are compensatory in nature and not punitive.

(2) The features that may attract an award of aggravated damages can be classified under three heads—(a) the manner in which the defendant has committed the tort; (b) the motive for it; and (c) the defendant's conduct subsequent to the tort but in relation to it.

(3) The features enumerated at (2) above affect the award of compensation because they aggravate the distress caused by the actual wrongful act.[165]

6.41 However, if the employment tribunal finds that the claim of indirect discrimination is successful but is satisfied that the PCP in question was not applied with the intention of discriminating against the complainant, it must not make an order of compensation *unless* it first considers whether to make an order of declaration or recommendation.[166]

---

[165] *Commissioner of Police of the Metropolis v Shaw [2012] ICR 464*, para. 16
[166] s124(4) and (5) of the Equality Act 2010

6.42 In discrimination cases, the amount to award a successful claimant for injury to feelings is gauged against the Vento Guidelines, which takes its name from the case *Vento v Chief Constable of West Yorkshire Police*.[167] The guidelines are updated annually, usually to take effect from April. The current updated guidelines from 6 April 2022 are, "In respect of claims presented on or after 6 April 2022, the Vento bands shall be as follows: a lower band of £990 to £9,900 (less serious cases); a middle band of £9,900 to £29,600 (cases that do not merit an award in the upper band); and an upper band of £29,600 to £49,300 (the most serious cases), with the most exceptional cases capable of exceeding £49,300."[168] In a case where a claimant has been dismissed, a basic schedule of loss may look something like the following:

6.43

[Heading – *Re: Stephanie*]
SCHEDULE OF LOSS
(As of 31 August 2021)

Date of termination of contract of employment: 30.4.21
Weekly salary (net): £315

---

[167] [2002] EWCA Civ 1871
[168] PRESIDENTIAL GUIDANCE Employment Tribunal awards for injury to feelings and psychiatric injury following *De Souza v Vinci Construction (UK) Ltd [2017] EWCA Civ 879*, 28 March 2022 https://www.judiciary.uk/wp-content/uploads/2013/08/Vento-bands-presidential-guidance-April-2022-addendum.pdf. See also 'Vento Guidelines for injury to feelings in discrimination cases' (https://youtu.be/B63SWxBzakc)

Monthly salary (gross): £1,775
Monthly salary (net): £1,365

(1) Loss of Earnings (Past to 31 August 2021):
Claimant has searched extensively to secure employment, of which she has provided evidence of in the bundle at pp. XXX

1 May to 31 August: £1,365 @ 4 months = **£5,460**

(2) Loss of Earnings (Future from 1 September 2021):
Claimant has now secured a job with ABCXYZ Ltd, which she is due to commence employment on 1 November 2021, earning the same as she did with the Respondent.

1 September to 31 October: £1,365 @ 2 months = **£2,730**

(3) Loss of Pension
The Respondent contributed 4% to Claimant's pension. Claimant will receive the same contribution under her new employment from 1 November, so there
is no loss after 31 October.

£1,775 @ 4% = £71 @ 6 months (May to Oct): **£426**

(4) Injury to feelings
The Claimant was and is deeply distressed by her dismissal. She was and is very hurt by Mr. Stan PP victimising her, simply for raising a grievance, which was her contractual right to do. Prior to her dismissal she was a confident and

outgoing person. She now suffers from a loss of confidence because of her being victimised by the Respondent. On this basis, the Claimant assesses her injury to feeling in the middle band of *Vento* at £18,100.

TOTAL LOSSES: £26,716 plus interest to be assessed by ET

Occasionally, the Respondent will produce a counter-schedule. A counter-schedule is not only useful to see the Respondent's position with respect to quantum, but it often highlights that there is little difference between the parties and it might encourage them to seek to settle their differences on a commercial basis. For example:

[Heading – *Re: Stephanie*]

COUNTER-SCHEDULE OF LOSS
(As of 31 August 2021)

(1) Loss of Earnings (Past to 31 August 2021):
Claimant has searched extensively to secure employment, of which she has provided evidence of in the bundle at pp. XXX

Respondent is of the view that the Claimant could have secured employment sooner. There are many vacancies in the area and had only received one request for a reference for the Claimant, which is the job she secured with ABCXYZ Ltd. The Respondent believes that the Claimant failed to mitigate her losses and should have secured a job to start no later than 1 July.

1 May to 30 June 31 August: £1,365 @ 4 2 months = £5,460 £2,730

(2) Loss of Earnings (Future from 1 September 2021): Claimant has now secured a job with ABC XYZ Ltd, which she is due to commence employment on 1 November 2021, earning the same as she did with the Respondent.
1 September to 31 October: £1,365 @ 2 months = £2,730

(3) Loss of Pension

The Respondent contributed 4% to Claimant's pension. Claimant will receive the same contribution under her new employment from 1 November, so there is no loss after 31 October.

£1,775 @ 4% = £71 @ 6 2 months (May to Jun): £426 £142

(4) Injury to feelings

The Claimant was and is deeply distressed by her dismissal. She was and is very hurt by Mr. Stan PP victimising her, simply for raising a grievance, which was her contractual right to do. Prior to her dismissal she was a confident and outgoing person. She now suffers from a loss of confidence because of her being victimised by the Respondent. On this basis, the Claimant Respondent assesses her injury to feelings in the ~~middle~~ lower band of *Vento*, at ~~£18,100~~ £2,500.

TOTAL LOSSES: £5,372 plus interest to be assessed by ET

Reconsideration and Appeal (EAT)

6.45 The scope of a full reconsideration and or an appeal (EAT, Court of Appeal, Court of Session and Supreme Court) is beyond the scope of this book. However, a tribunal may, either on its own initiative or on the application of a party, reconsider any judgment where it is necessary in the interests of justice to do so. On reconsideration, the original decision may be confirmed, varied or revoked. If it is revoked the decision may be taken again. Except where it is made in the course of a hearing, an application for reconsideration shall be presented in writing within 14 days of the date on which the written record, or other written communication, of the original decision was sent to the parties or within 14 days of the date that the written reasons were sent (if later) and shall set out why reconsideration of the original decision is necessary.[169]

6.46 Notwithstanding the process regarding a reconsideration, the period within which an appeal to the EAT may be instituted is– (a) in the case of an appeal from a judgment of the employment tribunal 42 days from the date on which

---

[169] r.70 and r.71 of the ET (Constitution & Rules of Procedure) Regs 2013, Sch. 1

the written reasons were sent to the parties.[170] Appeals lie, "only on a "question of law,"[171] the parties must expect any decision of fact made by an Employment Tribunal…to be decisive. It is not an error of law for a Tribunal, judge…to reach a decision which one party to the case thinks should have been differently made. The appeal is not a rehearing of the case. The Employment Tribunal must be shown to have made an error of law."[172]

6.47 An appellant who claims that there is an error of law must establish one of three things. Firstly, they must establish that the tribunal misdirected itself in law or misunderstood the law, or misapplied the law; or, secondly, that the tribunal misunderstood the facts, or misapplied the facts; or, thirdly the decision was "perverse," in that there was no evidence to justify the conclusion which they reached – in other words no reasonable tribunal even after having directed itself properly on the law could have arrived at the finding or conclusion it reached.

---

[170] r3(3)(a) of the Employment Appeal Tribunal Rules 1993
[171] s.21(ge) of the Employment Tribunals Act 1996 – "An appeal lies to the Appeal Tribunal on any question of law arising from any decision of, or arising in any proceedings before an employment tribunal under or by virtue of the Equality Act 2010."
[172] PD 2.1 and 2.2 of Practice Direction (Employment Appeal Tribunal - Procedure) 2018

~ CHAPTER SEVEN ~

"Often acts of discrimination are due to prejudice, to ignorance or to irrational repulsion, and those can be removed only by education or experience."
Mr Archibold Fenner Brockway, MP[173]

---

[173] 12 June 1956 at the House of Commons. See Chapter One, "How it all began"

DIVERSITY AWARENESS & INCLUSION

7.1 In some respects, I have left the most challenging for last. Strictly speaking, this heading is not entirely related to the preceding chapters, but, I would argue, it is not entirely unrelated either. The reader can pass judgment at the end and make up their own mind. This chapter seeks to demonstrate why, in my view, companies should embrace our differences, promote a more diverse workforce and enable an inclusive workforce at all levels right up to management and the boardroom.

7.2 I have read many books and articles on diversity awareness and inclusion, and like a judge sifting through a plethora of cases to arrive at the current state of case law, I have attempted to do the same over the years. From those that I have read, the moral (addressing the issue of *right* and *wrong*), underrepresentation (disproportionate representation compared with the relevant racial demographics), missed opportunities (missing out on a potentially wider and diverse pool of talent who can bring something new and fresh to the organisation to help gain that competitive advantage) *and* the obvious economic arguments in favour of inclusion stand heads above the others. To be clear, I don't claim this to be an exhaustive list or to be in order of importance.

7.3 Having looked at and agreed with what I have read over the years, I have concluded that there are many books that cover those areas far more eloquently than I would or could say myself and recommend that readers find material that suits them. I have chosen to take a route that has intrigued me for some time. As I stated in a podcast recently, for me, generally, diversity awareness is one of observation whilst inclusion is more of implementation. The latter seems harder for some to action than the former is to observe. In other words, it is easy to say that 'we have an underrepresentation.' The answer to the question, 'what are we going to do about it?' is where *more* work clearly needs to be done.

7.4 This book is about race relations and employment law and is not, primarily about diversity awareness and inclusion. However, I am a firm believer that with a diverse and inclusive workforce comes better employer and employee relations. And with this comes a better and more productive workforce. Colleagues who hear and read that their employer practises equality of opportunity are more likely to believe in this concept and act upon it accordingly when they witness this an action – from theory to action. When such evidence is on display, practising employers are more likely than not to attract from a wider pool 'all' the best talent available, and not simply the same with the same types of ideas. I like to think that innovation comes from all of us not just a few from one sector of society, so it is hard to comprehend why many organisations would choose to close their door to a vast diverse pool of such human resources simply because some people are deemed or perceived to be vastly different. So, I start with briefly exploring how *similar* we are before addressing the core issue of the extent of the diversity of which we are asked to be aware. When we get to this point of awareness, we then look at what we could or should do to address any perceived or actual lack of diversity in the workforce.

Social Construct

7.5　In Chapter Two we spoke about the social construct of 'race.' Racial classifications are not new. An 18th Century botanist had four categories of racial groups to which I shall not refer as these were later discredited but their effects have been long lasting. The reader can guess who was stated as being at the top and the bottom. Today, we are more enlightened. Today, we know as a fact that as a race there is *one* human race; there are *not* two or more. Today, we know as a fact that 99.9% of all humans' DNA is the same. From this we know that from the one race to which we all belong there is 0.1% difference in our DNA. Therefore, anywhere in the world, let alone in the workplace, a worker will be working alongside someone who is *significantly* and *substantially* more like them than they may care to know or believe. Moreover, it follows that one person is as equally or as much diverse as the next person with whom they wish to compare. In other words, what is deemed or perceived to be different and or diverse in Person X when compared with Person Y is *equally* different and or diverse in Y when compared with Person X. Therefore, from whichever perspective one chooses to view diversity, I would argue that *all* roads head and lead to the need for *all* to respect and embrace *all* our differences.

7.6 We saw from Dr Jones' example about the female from Virginia who, remarkably, appeared to be of either both the socially constructed race or, paradoxically, of neither. We see that it is conceivable to be of a legally constructed race under the Equality Act 2010 with the definition that race, "*includes*—(a) colour; (b) nationality; (c) ethnic or national origins,"[174] but not under one of its predecessors, the Race Relations Act 1976 (Amended) where racial grounds, "*means* any of the following grounds, namely colour, race, nationality or ethnic or national origins," and, racial group, "*means* a group of persons defined by reference to colour, race, nationality or ethnic or national origins, and references to a person's racial group refer to any racial group into which he falls." Therefore, we have a situation where a claimant may not have been deemed to belong to a *legal* racial ground prior to 1 October 2010 but belonged to one from that date.

7.7 The above are examples of why diversity and awareness training could and should be as wide as necessary to cover *all* persons irrespective of restrictions placed on various (social, legal and others) constructions, which are there to serve specific purposes and agenda.

Inclusion

7.8 "[E]mployers who use positive action measures may find this brings benefits to their own organisation or business. Benefits could include: a wider pool of talented, skilled and

---

[174] s.9(1) of the Equality Act 2010

experienced people from which to recruit; a dynamic and challenging workforce able to respond to changes; a better understanding of foreign/global markets; a better understanding of the needs of a more diverse range of customers – both nationally and internationally."[175]

7.9 Positive discrimination in Britain is unlawful, but positive action to address inclusion is not. In June 2021, the BBC was reported as being 'under fire,' for, "advertising a one-year, £17,810 trainee production management assistant role with the position "only open to black, Asian and ethnically diverse candidates"."[176] Under the Equality Act 2010, if an organisation reasonably thinks that—(a) persons who share a protected characteristic suffer a disadvantage connected to the characteristic, (b) persons who share a protected characteristic have needs that are different from the needs of persons who do not share it, or (c) participation in an activity by persons who share a protected characteristic is disproportionately low, the 2010 Act does not prohibit the organisation from taking any action which is a proportionate means of achieving the aim of—(a) enabling or encouraging persons who share the protected characteristic to overcome or minimise that disadvantage,(b) meeting those needs, or (c) enabling or encouraging persons

---

[175] Equality Act 2010 Code of Practice, para. 12.10
[176] Evening Standard (https://www.standard.co.uk/news/uk/bbc-discrimination-row-advertising-job-ethnic-monorities-b941600.html); Mail Online (https://www.dailymail.co.uk/news/article-9704235/BBC-sparks-discrimination-row-banning-white-people-applying-18-000-trainee-job.html)

who share the protected characteristic to participate in that activity.[177]

7.10 If an organisation reasonably thinks that—(a) persons who share a protected characteristic suffer a disadvantage connected to the characteristic, or (b) participation in an activity by persons who share a protected characteristic is disproportionately low, the 2010 Act does not prohibit the organisation from treating person (A) more favourably in connection with recruitment or promotion than another person (B) because A has the protected characteristic but B does not with the aim of enabling or encouraging persons who share the protected characteristic to—(a) overcome or minimise that disadvantage, or (b) participate in that activity. However, this applies only if—(a) A is as qualified as B to be recruited or promoted, (b) the organisation does not have a policy of treating persons who share the protected characteristic more favourably in connection with recruitment or promotion than persons who do not share it, and (c) taking the action in question is a proportionate means of achieving the aim to overcome or minimise that disadvantage, or participate in that activity.[178] Examples of, "disadvantage," may include, "exclusion, rejection, lack of opportunity, lack of choice and barriers to accessing employment opportunities."[179]

---

[177] s.158 of the Equality Act 2010
[178] s.159 (1) to (4) of the Equality Act 2010
[179] Equality Act 2010 Code of Practice, para. 12.16

7.11 Recruitment means a process for deciding whether to, among other things, offer employment to a person; make contract work available to a contract worker; offer a person a position as a partner in a firm or proposed firm; offer a person a position as a member of an LLP or proposed LLP; or offer a person a service for finding employment.[180]

7.12 Note that the positive action allowed under the 2010 Act does not enable an organisation to do anything that is prohibited by or under another enactment other than the 2010 Act.[181]

7.13 Some organisations are clearly placed better geographically to recruit a more diverse workforce than others. However, that should not prevent others who are not so well place to seek to address this if it "reasonably thinks that" positive action is necessary for reasons given above. "Six examples of positive action are placing job adverts to target particular groups, to increase the number of applicants from that group; including statements in job adverts to encourage applications from under-represented groups, such as 'we welcome female applicants'; offering training or internships to help certain groups get opportunities or progress at work; offering shadowing or mentoring to groups with particular needs; hosting an open day specifically for under-represented groups to encourage them to get into a particular field; favouring the job candidate from an under-

---

[180] s.159 (5) of the Equality Act 2010
[181] s.159 (6) of the Equality Act 2010

represented group, where two candidates are 'as qualified as' each other.[182]

7.14 As recently as 1 September 2021, The Guardian in the United Kingdom reported, "Black men who were junior surgeons in 2010 were 27% less likely to be promoted to consultant than white men between 2016 and 2020, while black women were 42% less likely. The stark evidence of a glass ceiling has raised warnings that treatment may suffer unless senior ranks are made more representative and "old boys' networks" dismantled. The Royal College of Surgeons described the study of more than 3,000 doctors as "deeply concerning"."[183] One cannot ignore that inclusion may necessarily involve a change in culture for some organisations. Changing ingrained attitudes, behaviours and cultures may not always have a smooth and easy transition. Notably, it is the subconscious mind that is one of the major mental forces behind a person's resistance to change. We shall discuss the notion of subconsciousness under Training in the next chapter. However, clearly, organisations will need to engage in and embrace fully the necessity for diverse inclusion in and within their workforce, which may entail further diversity awareness and training for its workforce.

---

[182] https://www.equalityhumanrights.com/en/advice-and-guidance/employers-what-positive-action-workplace
[183] Black surgeons 'promoted far less than white colleagues in England' (https://www.theguardian.com/society/2021/sep/01/black-surgeons-promoted-far-less-than-white-colleagues-in-england)

~ CHAPTER EIGHT ~

"[The] concept of institutional racism which we apply consists of [the] collective failure of an organisation to provide an appropriate and professional service to people because of their colour, culture, or ethnic origin."

The Macpherson Report [184]

---

[184]

https://assets.publishing.service.gov.uk/government/uploads/system/uploads/attachment_data/file/277111/4262.pdf, para 6.34

8.1 The term, 'institutional racism,' was not written about in the first edition of this book, which was published on 1 September 2021 in paperback and on 3 September 2021 on Kindle. It was a conscious decision because, as confirmed by the EAT, "There is no statutory or other offence consisting of a body being institutionally racist."[185] However, since its publication the term has been in the headlines for a variety of reasons. In fact, just a few days before the planned publication of the second edition of this book, a senior nurse who was employed by NHS England and NHS Improvement Commissioning as a continuing healthcare manager won her case of, amongst other things, discrimination because of race and harassment related to race and reportedly said, "It sadly proves that institutional racism is still present in organisations, despite the efforts to make it more inclusive for people of all races and backgrounds."[186] Sadly, as recently as 21 March 2023, Baroness Louise Casey of Blackstock who undertook an independent review into the Metropolitan Police's culture and standards following Sarah Everard's murder,[187] said, 'she felt not enough had changed since the 1999 Macpherson report, published after the murder of black teenager Stephen Lawrence, which labelled the Met

---

[185] *Commissioners of Inland Revenue and another (appellants) v Morgan (respondent) [2002] IRLR 776*

[186] https://www.nursingtimes.net/news/leadership-news/senior-nurse-wins-landmark-race-discrimination-case-against-nhs-24-02-2023/ and https://assets.publishing.service.gov.uk/media/63f393008fa8f5612d615da4/Ms_A_Cox_v_NHS_Commissioning_Board_-_2415350_2020___Other.pdf

[187] https://www.bbc.co.uk/news/uk-58833349

"institutionally racist" - a problem the force is "yet to free itself from".'[188]

8.2 Unbeknown to me at the time of writing the first edition in the summer of 2021, Yorkshire County Cricket Club was embroiled in a dispute over allegations of, amongst other things, institutional racism, which hit the headlines when Mr. Azeem Rafiq appeared before and gave testimony to the digital, culture, media and sport committee on 16 November 2021[189] and 13 December 2021.[190] I shall return to this.

8.3 Contrary to what might be popular belief, the term or concept of 'institutional racism' did not originate in either of the Scarman or Macpherson Reports of 1981 and 1999 respectively, which we discuss in this chapter. As early as 1967, Carmichael and Hamilton, referring to America, wrote, "Institutional racism relies on the active and pervasive operation," of, "attitudes and practices," and, "[Racism] permeates the society, on both the individual and institutional level, covertly and overtly."[191]

8.4 Let us remind ourselves of a definition given of 'institutional racism' given in The Macpherson Report:

---

[188] https://www.bbc.co.uk/news/uk-65015479, https://www.theguardian.com/uk-news/2023/mar/21/metropolitan-police-institutionally-racist-misogynistic-homophobic-louise-casey-report
[189] https://committees.parliament.uk/oralevidence/3012/pdf/
[190] https://committees.parliament.uk/oralevidence/12444/pdf/
[191] Black Power: The Politics of Liberation in America by Stokely Carmichael and Charles V. Hamilton (Vintage, 1967), p.4

Taking all that we have heard and read into account, we grapple with the problem. For the purposes of our Inquiry the concept of institutional racism which we apply consists of:

The collective failure of an organisation to provide an appropriate and professional service to people because of their colour, culture, or ethnic origin. It can be seen or detected in processes, attitudes and behaviour which amount to discrimination through unwitting prejudice, ignorance, thoughtlessness and racist stereotyping which disadvantage minority ethnic people.

Crown Prosecution Service in 2001

8.5 In July 2001, following the publications, The Denham Report – Race discrimination in the Crown Prosecution Service and CRE report on the Crown Prosecution Service's Croydon branch, "The director of public prosecutions, David Calvert-Smith, […] accepted that the crown prosecution service (CPS) was "institutionally racist." "Without intending to be, our behaviour can, does and has discriminated […] "Therefore I unreservedly accept the finding that as an organisation the CPS has been, within the Lawrence report definition, institutionally racist."[192]

8.6 In an article that appeared in The Guardian a year later, Mr. Hugo Young wrote, "Last year [Sir David] caused a stir by

---

[192] https://www.theguardian.com/uk/2001/jul/26/race.world2

saying his own organisation, the crown prosecution service, was institutionally racist. Now he's moving on, with a familiar refrain. If the CPS is guilty, so are we all guilty – but there's more. He claimed that the CPS, far from being culpable, is positively heroic, as are the police: for the CPS (through him) and the police (through their response to the Macpherson report on Stephen Lawrence) have owned up to being racist, whereas the people have not. The "people", says the DPP, are "institutionally racist". It was time they understood as much. This was, for a start, a revealing illiteracy. How can "people" be "institutionally" anything? People are not an institution."[193] As part of his evidence before the digital, culture, media and sport committee on 16 November 2021, Mr. Rafiq said of Yorkshire Cricket Club, "Suddenly, it felt like it went away from the institutional and, working with the club, they tried to make it about individuals." So, where does this leave us so far? Institution, individuals or both? If both, which 'individuals' would be blameworthy, culpable etc? Solely those responsible for the 'processes, attitudes and behaviour' of the institution in question or will all 'individuals' pay the price?

8.7 In his book, 'The Uncomfortable Truth About Racism,' the former England international footballer, John Barnes, addressed what it means when we say that an institution is institutionally racist. He says, "But that statement doesn't truly make sense, for an institution has no power alone. It's the people that give it power." He goes on to make the point that, "people bring their ideals and values into the

---

[193] https://www.theguardian.com/world/2002/jun/25/race.equality

institution they enter," because before they became members of those institutions they were, "members of society."[194] So, not only is there no universally accepted definition of institutional racism, but some may well question whether an institution deemed to be racist when measured against, say, the Macpherson version makes sense in any case.

Independent review into racism in Scottish cricket - 2022

8.8 Following the wide media attention surrounding the allegations at Yorkshire County Cricket Club, "one question hung over cricket, *"Could there be racism anywhere else in the game?"* Scottish cricketers began to share their stories and experiences of racism, pushing the focus onto Cricket Scotland. This led to **sport**scotland, the national agency for sport, instigating an independent review into racism in Scottish cricket."[195]

8.9 The review was led by equality, diversity, and inclusion specialists that developed a set of 31 indicators in relation to, "processes, attitudes, and behaviours," based on the Macpherson definition. The 31 indicators are as follows: (1) Leadership leads on, is accountable, and responsible for tackling racism; (2) Transparency is evident in decision-making at all levels; (3) Effective EDI Champion at Board

---

[194] Part One, Chapter 3, "Is football institutionally racist?" https://www.audible.co.uk/pd/The-Uncomfortable-Truth-About-Racism-Audiobook/1472290410

[195] https://sportscotland.org.uk/media/7801/changing-the-boundaries-independent-review-into-racism-in-scottish-cricket-report.pdf, p.4

level; (4) Open, inclusive, and transparent recruitment and appointment processes; (5) People from ethnically and culturally diverse communities in positions of authority, decision-making, and leadership; (6) Policies and procedures are followed and monitored for effectiveness; (7) EDI policies are reflective and complementary of safeguarding policies; (8) Meaningful anti-racism and EDI data is collected and acted on; (9) Inappropriate and discriminatory language is effectively challenged and addressed; (10) The organisation keeps up to date with changes in language relating to racism; (11) A culture of banter involving racially aggravated language is not normalised; (12) Younger players are not exposed to inappropriate language or behaviour in a senior match environment; (13) There is widespread agreement on what is discriminatory behaviour; (14) People's cultural and religious commitments or practises are anticipated, respected, and supported; (15) Dated or damaging stereotypes are not heard in cricket; (16) People from ethnically and culturally diverse communities are treated the same as others; (17) Processes for reporting racism are clear and communicated widely; (18) Proportionate number of people from ethnically diverse communities in the on-field, and off-field disciplinary system; (19) Allegations are investigated thoroughly and in a timely manner; (20) Micro-aggressions that are racially aggravated did not occur; (21) Racially aggravated bullying or harassment, does not happen; (22) Selection processes for talent pathways or representative squads are fair and transparent; (23) Criticism, scrutiny, and challenge are welcomed, and feedback is acted on; (24) Racism on social media relating to cricket is addressed or absent; (25) Education on racism, racial inequalities, and inappropriate language and behaviour is in place; (26) Ethnically and culturally diverse communities receive the same treatment in the media or through communications; (27) Ethnically and culturally diverse communities are consulted, and their views are listened to and acted on; (28) There is a welcoming environment and culture in cricket for ethnically and culturally diverse communities; (29) Proactive allyship advances a culture of anti-racism and inclusion; (30) The intersectionality of a person's race and other characteristics is not a barrier in cricket; and (31) Affinity bias is addressed and absent.[196]

8.10 Against each of the 31 indicators would be a colour rating/status as follows: Red status explained as, 'Document doesn't exist or not provided; Amber status explained as, 'Document in place but no mention of anti-racism or EDI; Green status explained as, 'Document in place and some mention of anti-racism or EDI however could improve or needs updating; and Blue status explained as, 'Document in place, anti-racism or EDI included to a good level and this is current.'[197]

8.11 There were, "almost 1000 direct engagements with people to hear their stories through face-to-face conversations and online, anonymous **Review of Racism in Scottish Cricket**

---

[196] https://sportscotland.org.uk/media/7801/changing-the-boundaries-independent-review-into-racism-in-scottish-cricket-report.pdf, pp. 11-12

[197] https://sportscotland.org.uk/media/7801/changing-the-boundaries-independent-review-into-racism-in-scottish-cricket-report.pdf, p.13

survey," over a 6-month period.[198] Out of the 31 indicators, 29 were given a red status (document doesn't exist or not provided) and 2 were given an amber status (document in place but no mention of anti-racism or EDI).[199] "From this analysis, 448 separate examples were identified that mapped against one of the **Plan4Sport Indicators of Institutional Racism**."[200] Therefore, in July 2022 it concluded that, "Having failed against 29 of the 31 indicators in the **Plan4Sport Indicators of Institutional Racism Framework**, the review would conclude that processes, attitudes, and behaviours of Cricket Scotland meet the Macpherson definition of institutional racism."[201]

London Fire Brigade - 2022

8.12 However, despite its having lasted the test of time, not all findings of alleged institutional racism need necessarily make any reference to Macpherson's version or any version for the headlines to label an institution as institutionally racist.[202] For example, in Nazir Afzal OBE's report, 'Independent Culture Review of London Fire Brigade,' which was published in November 2022,[203] it found that,

---

[198] https://sportscotland.org.uk/media/7801/changing-the-boundaries-independent-review-into-racism-in-scottish-cricket-report.pdf, p.4

[199] https://sportscotland.org.uk/media/7801/changing-the-boundaries-independent-review-into-racism-in-scottish-cricket-report.pdf, p.34

[200] https://sportscotland.org.uk/media/7801/changing-the-boundaries-independent-review-into-racism-in-scottish-cricket-report.pdf, p.33

[201] https://sportscotland.org.uk/media/7801/changing-the-boundaries-independent-review-into-racism-in-scottish-cricket-report.pdf, p.35

[202] https://news.sky.com/story/london-fire-brigade-is-institutionally-misogynist-and-racist-independent-review-finds-12755585

[203] https://www.london-fire.gov.uk/media/7211/independent-culture-

without reference to Macpherson, "Sadly, the majority of BAME staff and women that we interviewed all reported institutional failures with regards to supporting equality and diversity duties. Examples included the lack of opportunity afforded to BAME staff particularly and women in comparison to their white counterparts in areas such as promotion and reporting racial harassment and sexual harassment."[204]

Yorkshire County Cricket Club

8.13 The following is based solely on information that was and or is in the public domain at the time of writing. Former cricketer at Yorkshire County Cricket Club, Mr. Azim Rafiq, who alleged racist behaviour at the Club during parts of his spell at the Club was reported as saying in *ESPNcricinfo*, which was published on 2 September 2020, "Do I think there is institutional racism? It's at its peak in my opinion. It's worse than it's ever been."[205] On 3 September 2020, the Club was reported to have, "begun a full investigation into allegations of institutional racism made by former captain Azeem Rafiq."[206] On or around 5 September 2020 the Club

---

review-of-lfb-report953f61809024e20c7505a869af1f416c56530867cb99fb946ac81475cfd8cb38.pdf

[204] pp.50-51. See also https://www.bbc.co.uk/news/uk-england-london-63749444

[205] https://www.espncricinfo.com/story/azeem-rafiq-was-on-brink-of-suicide-after-experiencing-racism-at-yorkshire-1231162. See also Wisden published on 17 August 2020, https://wisden.com/stories/interviews/the-extraordinary-life-of-azeem-rafiq

appointed a law firm to lead the investigation into the allegations.[207] "The report, which took 12 months to complete and remains unpublished, upheld seven of his 43 allegations and accepted he had faced "racial harassment and bullying". Yorkshire announced last week that no current employees would face action as a result."[208] On 5 November 2021 the Club's Chairman, Mr. Roger Hutton, resigned, "ahead of an emergency meeting to discuss the club's response to racism experienced by former player Azeem Rafiq…An investigation found Rafiq was a victim of racial harassment and bullying – but the club said it would take no disciplinary action."[209] In his resignation statement, Mr. Hutton is reported as saying, 'there has been "a constant unwillingness from the executive members of the Board and senior management at the Club to apologise, and to accept that there was racism, and to look forward" over the affair.'[210] Mr. Hutton was replaced immediately by Lord Kamlesh Patel of Bradford, who was, "appointed as a director and chair of the Club."[211] On 16 November 2021 Mr. Rafiq, Mr. Hutton and Lord Patel appeared before and gave testimonies to the digital, culture, media and sport

---

[206] https://www.thecricketer.com/topics/yorkshire/yorkshire_investigation_azeem_rafiq_racism_allegations.html
[207] https://www.bbc.co.uk/sport/cricket/54041229
[208] https://www.theguardian.com/sport/2021/nov/05/key-players-involved-in-yorkshire-ccc-racism-scandal-cricket
[209] https://www.skysports.com/cricket/news/12040/12460414/yorkshire-county-cricket-club-chairman-roger-hutton-submits-resignation-over-handling-of-azeem-rafiq-racism-case
[210] https://www.yorkshirepost.co.uk/news/politics/yorkshire-ccc-chairman-roger-hutton-resigns-over-azeem-rafiq-racism-scandal-3445976
[211] https://www.itv.com/news/calendar/2021-11-05/yorkshire-appoints-bradford-lord-as-new-chair-as-cricket-racism-row-continues

committee Chaired by Mr. Julian Knight MP. I now pick up from where I left off above.

Digital, Culture, Media and Sport Committee – 16 November 2021

8.14   As part of his evidence, Mr. Rafiq said, "Clearly, the words "institutional racism" are something no one wants to be associated with." He said the investigators, "were brilliant, they were lovely at the start—so respectful, wanted to hear everything I had to say." But, "as soon as they got my evidence it felt like they were like, "Wow, we have a problem here." Suddenly, it felt like it went away from the institutional and, working with the club, they tried to make it about individuals. That is why, unfortunately, in the last couple of weeks some individuals have had a really tough time. I did not present my evidence like that. It was never intended like that and that was never the allegation, but that is what the club, the lawyers and the panel in particular have tried to do."[212]

8.15   Mr. Damian Green MP, said to Mr. Rafiq, "I take the point that you want to talk about the institution rather than the individuals, but recently [JR] has said in response to this that he can say that at no stage has he heard any racist conversations in the dressing room or around Yorkshire. Do you find that statement credible?" Mr. Rafiq replied, "To be clear, [JR] is a good man. He has never engaged in racist language […] it just shows—and he might not

---

[212] https://committees.parliament.uk/oralevidence/3012/pdf/ - Q4

remember it—how normal it was in that environment, in that institution, that even a good man like him does not see it for what it is. It was strange but, like I said, it is the environment of the institution that made it such a norm that people do not remember it. It is not going to affect [JR]. It is something I remember every day but I do not expect [JR] to."[213]

8.16 The following are questions put by Mr. Kevin Brennan MP to and answers given by Mr. Hutton and Lord Patel.[214]

Kevin Brennan: Mr Hutton, is Yorkshire Cricket Club institutionally racist?

Roger Hutton: The report concluded there was insufficient evidence. The panel concluded that there was insufficient evidence. I have to observe that in the last few months there has been a substantial amount of thoughtlessness and ignorance, a reluctance to apologise, a reluctance to see Azeem as the victim, and a reluctance to put into place the recommendations, which I think are really important in this process.

Kevin Brennan: That sounds to me like you are edging towards the word "yes" in answer to my question. Would that be fair?

Roger Hutton: I think the question remains unanswered.

Kevin Brennan: My question is to you rather than what happened in the report; in your view? You were chair for 18

---

[213] https://committees.parliament.uk/oralevidence/3012/pdf/ - Q25
[214] https://committees.parliament.uk/oralevidence/3012/pdf/ - Qs138-141

months and you have resigned.

Roger Hutton: Yes, I fear that it falls within that definition.

Kevin Brennan: Thank you. Lord Patel, how does it feel to be the chair of an organisation that is institutionally racist, according to its previous chair?

Lord Patel: That is a very interesting question.

Kevin Brennan: That is why I asked it.

Lord Patel: I suppose that almost suggests that organisations I have chaired in the past or that other people have chaired in the past are not institutionally racist and there is an issue. I have been appointed because there is a charge of institutional racism, and clearly the processes, the systems and the systemic nature of what has been going on, as we have witnessed in many organisations, feels to be there. My job is to work as hard as I can with people to change that process. I have to be proud of the organisation I am chairing, there is no question about that. I have to lead it into the right direction.

8.17 I leave it to readers to make up their own minds on what precisely had Mr. Hutton admitted to and how, "Yes, I fear that it falls within that definition," formed the basis of the question, "Lord Patel, how does it feel to be the chair of an organisation that is institutionally racist, according to its previous chair?" I also leave it to readers to decipher what Lord Patel meant by, "I suppose that almost suggests that organisations I have chaired in the past or that other people have chaired in the past are not institutionally racist and there is an issue."

Digital, Culture, Media and Sport Committee – 13 December 2021

8.18 On 13 December 2021 Lord Patel; Mr. George Dobell, cricket journalist; Mr. Jahid Ahmed, former Essex County Cricket Club cricketer; and Mr. Rafiq appeared before the digital, culture, media and sport committee, Chaired by Ms. Julie Elliott MP. During this hearing, Mr. Dobell stated, amongst other things, "[Institutional racism] is when the systems of power stand shoulder to shoulder to prevent change, to prevent justice. The systems of power include the media, absolutely they do."[215]

"Suddenly, it felt like it went away from the institutional and, working with the club, they tried to make it about individuals."

8.19 In November 2021 fourteen members of staff at Yorkshire County Cricket Club, "wrote a collective letter to [Mr.] Hutton and the board, drafted over six weeks, in a desperate attempt to outline their concerns and to put their side of the story."[216] On 3 December 2021 all 14 (plus two others) were either dismissed or, in consequence, had their contracts terminated by the club, following which some presented

---

[215] https://committees.parliament.uk/oralevidence/12444/pdf/ - Q737
[216] https://www.yorkshirepost.co.uk/sport/cricket/revealed-full-letter-from-sacked-yorkshire-ccc-staff-over-azeem-rafiq-affair-that-led-to-all-14-losing-their-jobs-3865957

complaints to the employment tribunal, which included, amongst other things, unfair dismissal.[217] On 23 May 2022, the Leeds Employment Tribunal published the judgment that, "The claimants' complaints of unfair dismissal are well founded."[218]

8.20 Following the said judgment, the club announced publicly: "On the 3rd December 2021 the Yorkshire County Cricket Club Limited took the decision to dismiss its coaching and medical staff. The club has acknowledged that its dismissals of that group of employees was procedurally unfair."[219]

8.21 In January 2023, Lord Patel announced that he was stepping down as Chair of Yorkshire County Cricket Club at the club's next AGM.[220]

England and Wales Cricket Board (ECB)[221] hearing 1-9 March 2023

8.22 "Yorkshire CCC has admitted liability in response to four amended charges, including a failure to address systemic use

---

[217] https://www.dailymail.co.uk/sport/cricket/article-10631227/Two-former-coaches-join-legal-fight-Yorkshire-following-mass-cull-staff.html
[218] https://assets.publishing.service.gov.uk/media/629f62d78fa8f5039a1bd721/Mr_I_Dews_and_Others_v_The_Yorkshire_Cricket_Club_LImited_-_1800858_2022_-_No_Hearing.pdf and https://www.bbc.co.uk/sport/cricket/61729326
[219] https://www.bbc.co.uk/sport/cricket/62909691
[220] https://www.skysports.com/cricket/news/12123/12781297/lord-kamlesh-patel-to-step-down-as-chair-of-yorkshire-county-cricket
[221] https://www.ecb.co.uk

of racist and/or discriminatory language over a prolonged period and a failure to take adequate action in respect of allegations of racist and/or discriminatory behaviour."[222]

Conclusion

8.23 Hiding behind the veil of Institutional Racism? There is a school of thought that says, unpleasant as it may appear, it is easier to confess to an institution being racist, of which some senior members (The Board, CEOs/MDs, SLTs etc) are part and who was responsible for the, "processes, attitudes and behaviour which amount to discrimination through unwitting prejudice, ignorance, thoughtlessness and racist stereotyping which disadvantage minority ethnic people," than it is for any of those individuals to take 'personal' responsibility. Many may resign but manage to 'escape' any personal liability, especially if such, 'processes, attitudes and behaviour which amount to discrimination,' were used to achieve, covertly, the desired discriminatory outcome. Cashmore tells of an American case in 1990 in which eight national major environmental organisations were charged with racism in their hiring practices. "In none of the attacks on the organizations were individuals singled out, nor were any motives imputed. No one was actually accused of refusing to appoint or promote anyone on racist grounds."[223]

---

[222] https://www.ecb.co.uk/news/3053026/update-on-charges-against-yorkshire-ccc-and-others

[223] *Dictionary of Race and Ethnic Relations, 4th Ed. (Routledge, 1996), pp.170-171*

8.24 There are numerous definitions, so it is important to recognise that any two people may have two entirely definitions in mind or, dare I say, two definitions that some may not even recognise as 'institutional racism' at all. On that basis, what might appear as institutionally racist to one may not appear so to another. In fact, what might appear as institutionally racist to one may be seen 'neutral' to another. For example, in responding to the suggestion that *"Britain is an institutionally racist society,"* Lord Scarman wrote in his report into the Brixton Riots of 1981, *"If, by [institutionally racist] it is meant that it [Britain] is a society which knowingly, as a matter of policy, discriminates against black people, I reject the allegation. If, however, the suggestion being made is that practices may be adopted by public bodies as well as private individuals which are unwittingly discriminatory against black people, then this is an allegation which deserves serious consideration, and, where proved, swift remedy."* (Para 2.22, p 11 - Scarman Report).[224] Some may argue that Lord Scarman's, *"If, however, the suggestion being made is that practices may be adopted by public bodies as well as private individuals which are unwittingly discriminatory against black people, then this is an allegation which deserves serious consideration, and, where proved, swift remedy,"* is not too dissimilar to the operation of indirect discrimination where a practice (PCP), which, on the face of it is neutral, is nevertheless, *'unwittingly discriminatory,'* in relation to a protected character (for our purposes, 'race'). "It would be possible to imagine a body whose habitual rules or practices were such that one could

---

[224] https://assets.publishing.service.gov.uk/government/uploads/system/uploads/attachment_data/file/277111/4262.pdf, para. 6.7. The Brixton Disorders, April 10-12, 1981: Inquiry Report. Lord Scarman: (Command Paper 8427)

fairly say of the body that as an institution it was racist. Forms of indirect discrimination would, perhaps, be the more likely to bring about some such case."[225]

8.25 It can be seen that the concept, understanding and identifying of institutional racism is not as straightforward as some may be led to believe. For example, the heavily criticised Sewel Report, to which I have already referred,[226] states, "...we also need clear, standard definitions of the terms institutional racism, structural racism or systemic racism. Right now they are used interchangeably..."[227] The Report goes on to make the following distinctions - **Institutional racism**: applicable to an institution that is racist or discriminatory processes, policies, attitudes or behaviours in a single institution; **Systemic racism**: this applies to interconnected organisations, or wider society, which exhibit Racist or discriminatory processes, policies, attitudes or behaviours. **Structural racism**: to describe a legacy of historic racist or discriminatory processes, policies, attitudes or behaviours that continue to shape organisations and societies today.[228]

---

[225] *Commissioners of Inland Revenue and another (appellants) v Morgan (respondent) [2002] IRLR 776, para.46*
[226] See 1.18
[227] https://assets.publishing.service.gov.uk/government/uploads/system/uploads/attachment_data/file/974507/20210331_-_CRED_Report_-_FINAL_-_Web_Accessible.pdf, p.35
[228] https://assets.publishing.service.gov.uk/government/uploads/system/uploads/attachment_data/file/974507/20210331_-_CRED_Report_-_FINAL_-_Web_Accessible.pdf, p.36

8.26 All the above brings us neatly to the point of when asked whether one believes that an institution is racist, we must first make sure that the communicating parties are on the same page. For example, let us look at the following exchange:

Exchange A

Mr. X: Mr Y, is Z institutionally racist?

Mr. Y: The report concluded there was insufficient evidence. The panel concluded that there was insufficient evidence. I have to observe that in the last few months there has been a substantial amount of thoughtlessness and ignorance, a reluctance to apologise, a reluctance to see Mr. B as the victim, and a reluctance to put into place the recommendations, which I think are really important in this process.

Mr. X: That sounds to me like you are edging towards the word "yes" in answer to my question. Would that be fair?

Mr. Y: I think the question remains unanswered.

Mr. X: My question is to you rather than what happened in the report; in your view?
You were chair for 18 months and you have resigned.

Mr. Y: Yes, I fear that it falls within that definition.

Mr. X: Thank you. **Mr. C**, how does it feel to be the chair of an organisation that is institutionally racist, according to its previous chair?

Exchange B

Mr. X: Mr Y, **based on D's definition of institutional racism**, is Z institutionally racist?

Mr. Y: The report concluded there was insufficient evidence. The panel concluded that there was insufficient evidence. I have to observe that in the last few months there has been a substantial amount of thoughtlessness and ignorance, a reluctance to apologise, a reluctance to see Mr. B as the victim, and a reluctance to put into place the recommendations, which I think are really important in this process.

Mr. X: That sounds to me like you are edging towards the word "yes" in answer to my question. Would that be fair?

Mr. Y: I think the question remains unanswered.

Mr. X: My question is to you rather than what happened in the report; in your view?
You were chair for 18 months and you have resigned.

Mr. Y: Yes, I fear that it falls within that definition.

Mr. X: Thank you. **Mr. C**, how does it feel to be the chair of an organisation that, according to its previous chair, **falls within W's definition of** institutionally racist?

Exchange C

Mr. X: Mr Y, **based on D's definition of institutional racism**, is Z institutionally racist?

Mr. Y: The report concluded there was insufficient evidence. The panel concluded that there was insufficient evidence. I have to observe that in the last few months there has been a substantial amount of thoughtlessness and ignorance, a reluctance to apologise, a reluctance to see Mr. B as the victim, and a reluctance to put into place the recommendations, which I think are really important in this process.

Mr. X: That sounds to me like you are edging towards the word "yes" in answer to my question. Would that be fair?

Mr. Y: I think the question remains unanswered.

Mr. X: My question is to you rather than what happened in the report; in your view?

You were chair for 18 months and you have resigned.

Mr. Y: Yes, I fear that it falls within that definition.

Mr. X: Thank you. **Mr. C**, how does it feel to be the chair of an organisation that is institutionally racist, according to its previous chair?

Mr. C: Respectfully, sir, the panel concluded that there was insufficient evidence. I cannot comment on what he *personally* observed in the last few months of his tenure. However, I am aware of the reports on Scottish Cricket and the London Fire Brigade that arrived at their conclusions after interviewing many people and basing their findings on the experience of many interviewees regarding certain processes, attitudes and behaviours. In consequence, I think it would be too much of a premature leap for me to say that Mr. Y's personal observation, based only 'in the last few months,' is enough for me to proclaim undeniably and unequivocally that the whole institution itself is racist without conducting further investigations and considering other personal observations of all stakeholders over a longer period of time than just, 'the last few months.' It is important that we get this right. For example, it would appear that *prior* to the last few months Mr. Y had not personally observed processes, attitudes and behaviours that would have led him to say that the institution was racist. Therefore, it is important that we establish what, if anything, has changed in the last few months and what processes, attitudes and behaviours, if any, have changed and why.

8.27 We can see from Exchanges A to C and throughout this chapter, it is important that the person to whom the question is put is given a definition that they understand or a definition on what the question is based. To do otherwise could lead to misunderstandings and an answer that does not accurately reflect the definition the questioner had in mind. In fact, in responding to Baroness Casey's report into the Metropolitan Police,[229] the head of the Metropolitan Police, Sir Mark Rowley, said, ""I don't use the 'institutional' label myself", arguing that the term is "ambiguous" and "politicised"."[230] After all, if the concept was objectively and universally understood it is doubtful that the Chair of The Inquiry into the matters arising from the death of Stephen Lawrence, Sir William Macpherson of Cluny, supported by Mr Tom Cook, The Rt. Revd Dr John Sentamu, Bishop for Stepney and Dr Richard Stone would have had the need to

---

[229] See 8.1
[230] https://www.bbc.co.uk/news/live/uk-65011583

interview many in order simply to arrive at the definition above, which, now, has stood the test of time.

8.27.1 An interesting case came before the EAT in 2011.[231] The Employment Tribunal found that both the respondents had directly discriminated against the claimant on the grounds of his race and that the employer had victimised him. The employment tribunal had concluded, amongst other things: ". . . at least in this segment of the First Respondent's organisation, what can only be described as **institutional, unconscious attitudinal racism**, at least in relation to persons of black African ethnicity; a corporate blindness to indications of racist thinking and to the possible implications of a complaint of race discrimination being raised in the context of a wider complaint of unfair or less favourable treatment" [**emphasis added**].

8.27.2 However, in allowing the appeal, the EAT held: "This finding was based on the failure to appreciate that the Respondent was raising race discrimination as a grievance, the lack of reaction to the "many mouths to feed" email, [Mr G's] "apparent blindness . . . to the racist implications of his own email" and the "complete lack of equality training". We do not think that this small collection of specific examples all relative to this case can justify the conclusion reached, even if it is confined to "this segment". **As in Morgan the Employment Tribunal has not defined the term "institutional racism".** The scope of the evidential material here cannot encompass "habitual

---

[231] *Transport for London v Aderemi (2011) UKEAT/0006/11*

rules and practices" (see para 46 of Morgan). In our judgment the evidential material simply cannot bear the weight of the structure erected above it," [**emphasis added**].

8.27.3 In the case of *Morgan*[232] to which the last paragraph refers, the EAT held: "**We are not saying that something reasonably describable as institutional racism can never be required to be examined into by tribunals. It would be possible to imagine a body whose habitual rules or practices were such that one could fairly say of the body that as an institution it was racist. Forms of indirect discrimination would, perhaps, be the more likely to bring about some such case.** But the charge would be relevant only as a step in the reasoning toward a conclusion that the body was or was not guilty of some unlawful discrimination that fell within the Act. In the case before us the charge, placed as it was, appears extraneous to the earlier-given conclusion. The sentence we have cited should not have appeared in the tribunal's extended reasons but, as an extraneous observation, it is not such, in our judgment, as of itself to vitiate the other conclusions at which the tribunal arrived," [**emphasis added**].[233]

8.28 To further complicate matters, there is no universal agreement that the concept of 'institutional racism,' is real. After all, an institution consists of individuals who make the decisions that are behind the existence of the institution's,

---

[232] *Commissioners of Inland Revenue and another (appellants) v Morgan (respondent) [2002] IRLR 776*
[233] Para.46

"processes, attitudes and behaviour which amount to discrimination through unwitting prejudice, ignorance, thoughtlessness and racist stereotyping which disadvantage minority ethnic people." Some of us might even recognise elements of 'unconscious bias' in, "...unwitting prejudice, ignorance..." and ask whether it is fair to label an intangible entity as an institution as 'racist' when compared to an individual who is overtly or covertly racist. Some of the more forensic among us might even question the use of conjunction 'and' in the definition, as in, "processes, attitudes <u>and</u> behaviour which amount to discrimination through unwitting prejudice, ignorance, thoughtlessness <u>and</u> racist stereotyping," and ask why not the use of 'or' in its place, as in, "processes, attitudes <u>or</u> behaviour<u>s</u> which amount to discrimination through unwitting prejudice, ignorance, thoughtlessness <u>or</u> racist stereotyping." Using 'or' in place of 'and' makes a big difference. Or, some might even want to use both, as in, 'and or.'

8.29 *I am part of 'X'. Therefore, I must be 'Y'?* Many years ago, I had cause to research one of the central questions addressed by Lord Scarman and the Sewel Report. That is, in the round, is a particular nation institutionally racist? Some may well ask, 'why is this question important?' After all, I am not a 'nation' and I am 'not' a racist. However, it is important to understand what it is people are addressing or think they are addressing when confronted with this question. Some may well think, if a nation was found to be institutionally racist, where does that leave a company or organisation when the people who 'are' and 'form part of' that nation 'are' and 'form part of' the workers of the company or organisation within that same nation? In other words, would attitudes in a wider society change in the workplace? No one will reasonably argue that everyone in a nation thinks alike, so how can one be tarnished with a brush of being 'institutionally racist' simply because they 'are' and 'form part of' a particular nation or they 'are' and 'form part of' the workers of a particular company or organisation? No one would reasonably suggest that South Africa during its apartheid era was a reflection or the product of the mindset of *all* South Africans! The point is, the employee who alleges that the institution of which they form part is 'institutionally racist' is not for one moment suggesting, unless they confess otherwise, that they are in any way a racist. It is not a case of 'X' is 'Y'. I am part of 'X'. Therefore, I must be 'Y.'

8.30 From the above discussions, cases, definitions and examples, institutional racism might be one of those terms that many can recognise in practice but few can define uniformly. In some cases, 'institutional discrimination' might be more of an accurate description of a particular circumstance. We do not believe that on each and every occasion a person found to have been unlawfully discriminated against because of their race was *necessarily* treated that way by an individual racist discriminator. That point can be extended to the company respondent. We do not believe that on each and every occasion a person found to have been unlawfully discriminated against because of their race was *necessarily* treated that way by an institutionally racist employer. Neither discrimination nor racism is attractive, but the latter might appear worse than the former in the minds of many.

8.31 An institution's processes, attitudes and or behaviours – in some way like indirect discrimination – might well have an adverse discriminatory effect on some. If so, change those processes, attitudes and or behaviours. However, when it comes to racism, on the other hand, this is not simply about amending policies that will *simply* have the effect of changing processes, attitudes and or behaviours. Here, we are talking about seeking, potentially, to change minds and, in some cases, ideologies of those who are *themselves responsible* for the institution's processes, attitudes and or behaviours. In that case, a root and branch change may well be required. If so, to achieve the desired outcome would appear to be a necessary root and branch change not of the workers within the institution as a whole but of those *responsible* for the institution's collective failure to provide an appropriate and professional service to people because of their colour, culture, or ethnic origin and its processes, attitudes and behaviours that amount to discrimination through unwitting prejudice, ignorance, thoughtlessness and racist stereotyping that disadvantage minority ethnic people.

8.32 I say this because, clearly, those who work within an institution labelled as institutionally racist are not culpable for the label simply because they work for or within that institution unless there is evidence against the individuals *personally* (on a case by case basis) to suggest otherwise. If X, who is a reputable civil rights campaigner, applies successfully to work for Y, labelled as institutionally racist after X works for it, it would be absurd to jump to the conclusion that X is somehow liable or blameworthy for this label based simply on X's being an employee of Y. I doubt that many of us would disagree. If the practice of Pearson Specter Litt LLC's is to employ graduates solely from Harvard, any quarrel that graduates from Yale (or elsewhere) has with that exclusionary policy and resultant processes, attitudes and or behaviours is not with the Harvard graduates who applied successfully to work there but with the partners responsible for adopting and implementing the policy itself. On that basis, there is a case for arguing that it is the partners *solely* who should be held to account.

Effect change

8.33 It seems to me that in order to change the processes, attitudes and or behaviours of an institution labelled as, 'institutionally racist,' one needs first to examine their policies, practices, processes, attitudes and or behaviours and seek to eliminate all effects of race discrimination and or the specific elements responsible for them. Unlike an employer who has written equal opportunities policies of which its employees are unaware or do not practice, it is important that an organisation practices what it claims to do. Macpherson's definition is used in many policies, which is evidence only that one is aware of it but not that one has taken any heed of it.

8.34 In an interview with Sky Sports News many years ago, barrister Mr. Peter Herbert OBE, 'The Chairman of the Society of Black Lawyers [had] accused the Football Association of "institutional racism",' about which he said he had, 'complained to the Minister of Sport about the FA.' It was put to him by the reporter, "You are accusing the Football Association of being institutionally racist?" to which he responded, "If an institution fails to follow 14 years after the Macpherson report's recommendations and it has a history of under-reporting racist hate, what would you call it? We would call it institutional racist."[234] Whether one shared Mr. Herbert's view or not, it is fair to say that 'football' has since taken steps to address many issues around diversity, inclusion[235] and race hate.[236] Whether it has gone far enough or fast enough I leave for others to debate.

8.35 Regarding cricket, following much of the above, the ECB reported, "We need to make cricket more inclusive – As the national governing body of cricket in England and Wales, we know that we must do more to make cricket an inclusive and welcoming sport. The brave and often distressing testimonies of racism and discrimination experiences in the game have been difficult to hear. The ECB established the Independent Commission for Equity in Cricket (ICEC),

---

[234] https://www.skysports.com/watch/video/sports/football/8247939/fa-labelled-institutionally-racist

[235] 'Football Leadership Diversity Code 2021/22 update' (https://www.premierleague.com/news/2877372)

[236] 'Premier League's No Room For Racism Action Plan' (https://www.premierleague.com/news/2021164)

which began work 2021 and is chaired by Cindy Butts. It was commissioned to report independently of the ECB on the state of equity in cricket. The ICEC is due to publish its findings in early 2023, and its recommendations will help shape the next EDI actions we take as a game."[237]

8.36 On 4 May 2022 Essex County Cricket Club was charged £50,000 by The Cricket Discipline Commission, which is the body that hears disciplinary cases in the professional domestic game of cricket in England and Wales (CDC) after it admitted two charges brought by the ECB. One was, 'the use of racist and/or discriminatory terminology,' by the then Chair of its Executive Board and General Committee at an Executive Board meeting on 7 February 2017. The other was, the failure of its Executive Board to conduct an appropriate, or any, investigation into whether or not the Chair had used the said terminology once the allegation of its use was known to all members of the Executive Board and General Committee in January 2018.[238] On 5 May 2022 Essex County Cricket Club published a statement that said, amongst other things, "The Club has a zero-tolerance policy towards racism and any form of discrimination. We continue to work with the ECB to eradicate discrimination from the game, which includes implementing their 12-point action plan and the Club's further commitment to Equity, Diversity & Inclusion (EDI) policies and processes."[239]

---

[237] Equity, Diversity and Inclusion (https://www.ecb.co.uk/about/equity-diversity-and-inclusion/overview)
[238] https://resources.ecb.co.uk/ecb/document/2022/05/05/6164e901-ef8e-423d-9bbe-f559aecb7ca4/CDC-Disciplinary-hearing-Essex-CCC.pdf
[239] https://www.essexcricket.org.uk/2022/05/05/club-statement-cricket-

8.37 Finally, therefore, regular audits and checks should be done to ensure that the effects of the new policies and practices do in fact achieve the lawful objective of equality of opportunities, respect and dignity at work. To be clear, I am referring *solely* to institutional racism and not where individuals are acting or have acted in an unlawful discriminatory manner or racially harassed another for which there are laws in place to deal with such unlawful behaviour and for which institutions are statutorily vicariously liable unless they are found to be otherwise.

8.38 In many cases, training is the beginning for change or a way of maintaining the institution's non-racist and or non-discriminatory processes, attitudes and or behaviours, and it is to this we turn to next and last.

discipline-commission-panel-decision/

~ CHAPTER NINE ~

"None of us is born intolerant of those who differ from us. Intolerance is taught and can be untaught."
United Nations Secretary-General, Kofi Annan[240]

---

[240] On receiving the Stephen P. Duggan award for international understanding from the Institute for International Education in New York on 27 November 2001

TRAINING

9.1 An applicant is shortlisted for a job and is called in for an interview. To make the applicant feel comfortable, the interviewer, a white female, goes to the reception area to meet and greet the interviewee, a black female. Other than the interviewee being a female, that she did not deem herself disabled and is highly qualified and suitable for the post, the interviewer knew little else about the candidate. However, without doubt or question, the interviewer is genuinely pleased to see the candidate and ushers her smiling into the conference room. After deciding not to sit at the head of the long oak table but opposite the candidate, the interviewer opens the conversation and the following exchange ensues:

Interviewer: Where are you from?

Interviewee: RC Legal Charity.

Interviewer: No, where do you come from?

Interviewee: We're based in Hackney.

Interviewer: No, what part of Africa are you from?

Interviewee: I don't know, they didn't leave any records.

Interviewer: Well, you must know where you're from, I spent time in France. Where are you from?

Interviewee: Here, the UK.

Interviewer: No, but what nationality are you?

Interviewee: I am born here and am British.

Interviewer: No, but where do you really come from, where do your people come from?

Interviewee: 'My people', lady, what is this?

Interviewer: Oh I can see I am going to have a challenge getting you to say where you're from. When did you first come here?

Interviewee: Lady! I am a British national, my parents came here in the 50s when...

Interviewer: Oh, I knew we'd get there in the end, you're Caribbean!

Interviewee: No lady, I am of African heritage, Caribbean descent and British nationality.

Interviewer: Oh so you're from...[241]

---

[241] https://www.bbc.co.uk/news/uk-63810468

9.2   The interviewer gladly offers the candidate the job, subject to satisfactory references. The interviewer happily returns to her office, thinking that was a job well done and looking forward to the interviewee commencing employment with her charity. The next day, the interviewee declines the offer.

9.3   Finally, therefore, I end with the importance of training. Employers need to ensure that their staff's training is regular, robust, relevant and up to date. For example, in Chapter One we saw the debates about the need for race relations legislation in the 1950s and 1960s. During those debates people were frequently referred to as 'coloured.' Today, such language would be unacceptable. However, one cannot ignore the fact that such language was *once* used and widely accepted – by whom is beyond the scope of this book. Acceptable and unacceptable language evolves. Take, for example, the opening of a 1982 Court of Appeal decision: "At the material time the appellant was a coloured English girl of the age of 19."[242] Today, our second highest appellate court would neither refer to a woman as a 'girl' nor 'coloured.' Therefore, simply repeating what has been taught annually may become stale, out of date and a tick box exercise rather than an engaging and learning exercise. As Mr Brockway MP said during the debate on 12 June 1956 where I began this book, "Often acts of discrimination are due to prejudice, to ignorance or to irrational repulsion, and those can be removed only by education or experience." [243]

---

[242] *Owen & Briggs v James (CA) [1982] ICR 618*
[243] Chapter One, 'How it all began.'

9.4 The obvious training to undertake is to train staff on the definitions of the key subject matters covered in this book, especially those relating to direct and indirect discrimination, racial harassment and victimisation. However, such training should not be limited *solely* to acts and behaviour done *consciously* but address also those done *subconsciously* and *unconsciously*.

9.5 "The mere fact that the claimant has been treated unfairly and that he comes from an ethnic minority does not constitute racial discrimination: it has to be shown that it was the claimant's race which was the reason why the discriminator discriminated. The whole question lies within the mind of the alleged discriminator. Thus the question is essentially a subjective one: why did the alleged discriminator act as he did?"[244]

9.6 To some extent discriminatory acts done consciously are easy to address in training than acts done subconsciously and unconsciously. If a worker consciously discriminated against another worker because of race, one ought to be able to engage with the discriminator to understand their motive(s) for behaving the way they did. The discriminator ought to be able to explain *their* rationale behind *their* actions. They ought to do this because they *consciously* thought about their actions *prior to* undertaking them. The same cannot be said for one's subconscious and unconscious behaviour.

---

[244] *Lord Browne-Wilkinson in Nagarajan (appellant) v. London Regional Transport (respondents) [1999] IRLR 572, para.6*

9.7 "I turn to the question of subconscious motivation. All human beings have preconceptions, beliefs, attitudes and prejudices on many subjects. It is part of our make-up. Moreover, we do not always recognise our own prejudices. Many people are unable, or unwilling, to admit even to themselves that actions of theirs may be racially motivated. An employer may genuinely believe that the reason why he rejected an applicant had nothing to do with the applicant's race. After careful and thorough investigation of a claim members of an employment tribunal may decide that the proper inference to be drawn from the evidence is that, whether the employer realised it at the time or not, race was the reason why he acted as he did. [...] Members of racial groups need protection from conduct driven by unrecognised prejudice as much as from conscious and deliberate discrimination. Balcombe LJ adverted to an instance of this in *West Midlands Passenger Transport Executive v Singh* [1988] IRLR 186, 188. He said that a high rate of failure to achieve promotion by members of a particular racial group may indicate that 'the real reason for refusal is a conscious or unconscious racial attitude which involves stereotyped assumptions' about members of the group."[245]

9.8 Many books treat subconscious and unconscious as one and the same. They are not. Many actions undertaken routinely do not always engage the conscious mind. How many times have we asked (or been asked), "Why do you/we do it that way?" and are met with an answer such as, "I don't know.

---

[245] *Lord Nicholls in Nagarajan (appellant) v. London Regional Transport (respondents) [1999] IRLR 572, para.17*

We have always done it that way!" Then the person thinks about it and gives an explanation. Or we routinely take the same route home by walking and chatting on the mobile phone without getting lost along the way. We may well be consciously engaged in our conversation on the mobile, but we are unlikely to be thinking about *how* to find our way home successfully. Our subconscious mind, which aided our routine journey home (stored in our memory), was the part of our mind that was *not at the time* in central awareness. The *Oxford Reference* describes subconscious as, "describing mental processes of which a person is not aware. [In psychoanalysis], denoting the part of the mind that includes memories, motives, and intentions that are momentarily not present in consciousness but can more or less readily be recalled to awareness."[246]

9.9 Behaviours done subconsciously and or routinely at work that calls into question an organisation's commitment to anti-discriminatory practices, equal opportunities and or diversity awareness and inclusion can be addressed in training as such behaviours, 'can more or less readily be recalled to awareness.' Therefore, seeking to change unacceptable behaviours in the workplace *necessarily* entails making workers become consciously aware of their actions that might previously have been acted upon subconsciously.

---

[246]

https://www.oxfordreference.com/view/10.1093/oi/authority.20110803100539429

9.10　Unconscious is arguably the hardest of the three (conscious, subconscious and unconscious) to check. By definition it is *un*conscious and not subject to the same examination as the other two. It is not in the memory to recall. The unconscious mind is shaped by many factors, experiences etc the moment we are born. You will have heard of 'unconscious bias,' which is a process by which we are *automatically* bias – for good or for bad – depending on a situation with which we are faced. The 'problem' we can have with unconscious bias is how can we prevent an unlawful discriminatory act if one's thought process is automatic. In other words, you are not conscious of the unconscious or unconscious bias. Here, we can see that a *special* type of training may be necessary. With the others – conscious and subconscious – one can train staff to be aware of their potentially discriminatory decisions and actions and to avoid them.

9.11　With unconscious bias introspection is not an option. Therefore, an organisation will need to have enough checks and balances in place – ideally involving more than one person – to seek to ensure that decisions and actions of which might have been influenced by the unconscious mind do not result in actions that amount to being unlawfully discriminatory or breaching policies such as equal opportunities, diversity awareness and inclusion etc.

9.12　Some organisations have anti-discrimination, equal opportunities and diversity and awareness training as part of their induction, which is all very well. However, sadly, that is often the only training staff receive on such matters throughout their whole working life at the organisation. This is simply not enough. It is suggested that *all* employees, irrespective of rank, attend regular and periodic refresher courses whether one feels they need to or not. Furthermore, organisations can also check and insist that workers, who are not their employees, have also undertaken such training recently. Organisations want to avoid acts of race discrimination, harassment related to race and victimisation being carried out by *those* working for it in *any* capacity and would equally want those workers to be protected from being subjected to such unlawful behaviour and conduct to ensure a better working environment for all.

9.13 We now turn to questions that may assist a training programme, but before we do that one should assume, despite the many offers of training on the subject, unconscious bias training is universally welcomed.

9.14 In a statement on 'Unconscious Bias Training' made by Ms. Julia Lopez MP on 15 December 2020, she wrote:

"Unconscious bias training typically aims to raise awareness of the potential biases and cognitive shortcuts that may negatively affect decision-making and behaviour in the workplace. The intent is usually to reduce both explicit and implicit bias towards members of particular groups that share characteristics protected under law and change behaviour.

"Although unconscious bias training takes a variety of forms, it is normally delivered as a discrete individual or group session that aims to set out the theory behind implicit bias, provide exercises that demonstrate how such biases might potentially affect behaviour, and suggest strategies to participants for avoiding that behaviour in future.

"Such training sessions have been introduced by a range of organisations as part of a well-intentioned effort to build fairer and more inclusive workplaces. They have often formed part of a wider employer toolkit aimed at tackling discrimination and building inclusion.

"However, in recent years a significant debate has emerged over their effectiveness and quality. Despite a growing diversity training industry and increased adoption of unconscious bias training programmes, a strong body of evidence has emerged that shows that such training has no sustained impact on behaviour and may even be counter-productive."[247]

9.15 Mr. Colin Prescod, the former chair of the Institute of Race Relations was reported as saying, "It's racism we want to talk about, it's systemic behaviour we want to talk about, institutionalised racism we want to talk about, not unconscious bias or racial awareness."[248]

---

[247] https://questions-statements.parliament.uk/written-statements/detail/2020-12-15/hcws652
[248] https://www.theguardian.com/world/2023/feb/18/unconscious-bias-training-is-nonsense-says-outgoing-race-relations-chair

9.16 *Questions*

1. Colin was born in St. Kitts. He applies for a job and is granted an interview. At the interview the interviewer says to Colin I can tell from your accent that you come from Tobago. He says he prefers Nevis and would have given Colin the job had he come from Nevis instead. Colin is therefore unsuccessful. Does Colin have a case?

2. Would your answer to 1 be different had the interviewer stated that he knew Colin was from St. Kitts and did not offer him the job because he prefers people from Nevis?

3. Would your answer to 1 be different had the interviewer stated that he knew Colin was from St. Kitts and did not offer him the job because he had 'an issue' with a Kittitian before?

4. Joy goes for an interview and reveals to the interviewer that she was thinking of taking her previous employer to the Employment Tribunal for direct race discrimination. The interviewer explains to Joy that but for thinking about suing her previous employer, he would have employed her. Does Joy have a case?

5. Would your answer to 4 be different had Joy already presented her complaint (as opposed to simply *thinking about it*)?

6. Winston defines himself as white and Peter defines himself as black. They both work for the same employer and have the same boss. One day their boss says something that Winston takes offence to as being related to Peter's race and was degrading. Winston raises a grievance, which is not upheld because Peter did not take offence to what their boss said. Does Winston have a case?

7. Would your answer to 6 be different had Peter also taken offence to the boss's remark?

8. Winston decides to sue the employer, but the employer says it should not be liable because it had warned their boss previously about similar banter, which they warned had occasionally been "over the top." Does the employer have a good defence?

9. Would your answer to 6 be different had Winston been engaged on a contract personally to do work and thus was not employed under a contract of employment?

10. Would your answer to 6 be different had the boss said the remark was a one-off and so could not possibly have known that Winston would not like it?

11. Lyra is from Ghana and defines herself as black. She has a 'natural' afro. She has worked for her employer as a receptionist for 2 days. On Day 1 she wore her favourite wig, which has hair that is straight and black. On Day 2 she went to work without her wig. Her boss commented that the company has a policy that afros are forbidden in the workplace (which is true). He demands that Lyra does not return to work with her afro again. She refuses to *return at all*. Does Lyra have a case?

12. Would your answer to 11 be different had Lyra worked in an environment that raised a potential health and safety risk?

13. Would your answer to 11 be different had Lyra's boss lied about the policy – in that there was no such Company policy – and it was discovered that he did not like it because it reminds him of the Civil Rights Movement in 1960s America?

14. Is there a difference between direct discrimination and indirect discrimination? If so, what is the difference?

15. Can the same facts give rise to a claim of both direct discrimination and indirect discrimination?

16. Is there a difference between direct discrimination and harassment? If so, what is the difference?

17. Can the same facts give rise to a claim of both direct discrimination and harassment?

18. To be protected from being victimised, does a worker solely have to use the word "discrimination" or the words "discriminated against" as part of their complaint?

19. Is "less favourable" treatment the same as "unfavourable" treatment?

20. Can an employer decide not to hear a grievance because the allegations of race discrimination are too trivial?

21. Kevin was not given the right to be accompanied by a fellow colleague or trade union representative during an investigation into an allegation that he racially harassed a colleague. He wants to claim race discrimination because of the employer's refusal. Does he have a case?

22. Pertaining to 21, Kevin was suspended during the investigatory process. He claims that his suspension amounts to less favourable treatment because of his race. Does he have a case?

23. Pertaining to 22, would your answer be any different if he alleged that his suspension amounted to unfavourable treatment?

24. Pertaining to 21 and 22, Kevin says he is being victimised. Does he have a case?

25. Pertaining to 24, would your answer be different had Kevin said he was being victimised because of his race?

26. Kevin was dismissed for allegedly racially harassing a colleague. He says his dismissal was an act of victimisation. When, if at all, did Kevin make a protected act?

27. Kevin notifies ACAS on 1 January 2021 about his dismissal on 1 June 2020. He says his hurt feelings stopped on New Year's Eve and so notified ACAS in good time of his pain stopping. Is Kevin's claim within time?

28. Pertaining to 27, would your answer be different had Kevin notified ACAS on 1 September 2020?

29. Pertaining to 27, would your answer be different had Kevin notified ACAS on 31 August 2020?

30. As part of his case, Kevin says that although he accepts that his conduct was unwanted by his colleague, it related to race and had the effect of creating an offensive environment for his colleague, that was not Kevin's purpose. Does Kevin have a good defence?

31. Pertaining to 30, would your answer be different if Kevin said it was not the conduct's purpose?

32. Pertaining to 30, would your answer be different if Kevin said it's his Employer's problem, not his?

33. Pertaining to 30, would your answer be different if Kevin said he has never been trained not to be racially offensive by his Employer?

34. Company X tells its staff that if they are caught racially discriminating against a colleague, "you are on your own." Does Company X have a good defence if taken to an employment tribunal for race discrimination?

35. Company Y says it would employ any applicant of Z ethnicity because Z ethnicity is underrepresented at the Company Y. Is this lawful?

36. Company Y says Z race is underrepresented at the Company Y and seeks to encourage applicants of Z race to apply. Is this lawful?

37. Eric from Company S goes out for an evening with his friends and is heard making racially offensive remarks by his colleague, Rhys, who complains to their boss the next day. Will Company S have grounds to discipline Eric for his conduct?

38. Pertaining to 37, does Rhys have a right to have his grievance heard by Company S?

39. Doreen says she was victimised by her boss last week because she told her boss that she discriminated against her. Does Doreen have a good case?

40. Ato says he was victimised by his boss, Harold, last week because he told Harold that he racially discriminated against him. Does Ato have a good case?

41. James says he was victimised by his boss, Anna, last week because he told Anna today that she racially harassed him. Does James have a good case?

42. Company M admits not favouring some people of U race of whom Belitta's partner, Sarah, belongs. Belitta describes herself as belonging to C race, whom Company M favours very much. However, Belitta is not invited to the Company party because she would bring Sarah. Does Belitta have a case?

43. Company B has an induction course for all Employees on their first day at work that covers Equal Opportunities, Diversity and Inclusion. Frank brings a case of harassment against Company B and Ishmail. Does Company B have a good statutory defence?

44. Company W decides not to hear Povey's grievance of racial harassment to avoid, "a culture of high sensitivity." Does Povey have a case?

45. Winston is dismissed because of a grievance of race discrimination was upheld against him. Is this good practice by his former employer?

46. A Colleague is not dismissed despite having a grievance of racial harassment against them. Is this good practice by his Employer?

47. Taariq considers bringing a claim of victimisation against Company S and wants to enter into a COT3 arrangement. Is this the correct arrangement?

48. Samuel and Company T agree to part ways and decide to enter into a settlement agreement. Is this the correct arrangement?

49. Company Y tells Kojo, during a "without prejudice" conversation, that they admit he was not promoted due to race. Kojo wants to refer to this part of the conversation at his forthcoming employment tribunal trial. Can he?

50. A PCP puts a class of people of Z at a particular disadvantage. Sinnita was not put at that disadvantage. Would Sinnita have a claim for race discrimination?

51. Pertaining to question 50, would your answer be different if Sinnita had suffered the disadvantage?

52. Afua raises a complaint of racial harassment and is offered internal mediation to resolve the issue by HR of Company B, which practices 'zero tolerance' with regard to discrimination. Would this be a fair process?

53. Pertaining to question 52, would your answer be different if Company B did not have a 'zero tolerance' policy?

54. Logan raises a complaint of race discrimination with his manager. His manager says, "leave it with me, I'll sort it out." What should the manager do next?

55. Somebody raises a complaint of victimisation and is offered internal mediation. The mediator suggests an outcome. Must the parties accept the suggested outcome?

56. A white, English person raises a complaint of race discrimination against their white English boss. The Company says the complainant can't claim race discrimination because the two are of the same race. Does the Employee have a case?

57. Pertaining to question 56, does the Employer have a good case?

58. Cara brings a case of racial harassment against her Employer and decides not to plead her full case in the ET1/Grounds of Complaint so that she can surprise her Employer with the evidence at trial. Is this a good idea?

59. Pertaining to question 58, would your answer be different subsequently if Cara's Employer were to admit to the 'surprise' evidence (racial harassment) at trial?

60. George gets notice of his hearing, which is 6 months away. He wants to amend his claim, which he believes is a simple 'relabelling' exercise. He decides not to make an application to amend until he is about to give his evidence. As he can apply to amend his claim at any time, advise George whether this is a good tactic.

61. Would your advice to George change if he told you that, leaving it so late to make his application is his main trump card to "wrong foot" the respondent?

62. Doris, who is black, goes for an interview for a local charity and is asked where she is from? She says she is from Scotland. The interviewer asks her where is she 'really' from? Doris says she is from Glasgow. The interviewer expresses surprise and says, 'You speak very well for your kind. You have the job.' Advise interviewer on his interviewing technique.

63. Would your advice change if the interviewer told you in confidence that he only asked Doris those questions because he loves to hear her kind speak with an accent, which makes her laugh?

64. Ruby is from Sudan and has worked for her employer for over 25 years. One day she asked her boss, Eric, why she has never been promoted and others far less experienced than her have. Her boss tells her that the company has never had, "you lot," in senior positions so why change it now? Advise Ruby on what she could do next.

65. Advise Eric on whether changes are required and why.

66. Would your advice change if Eric tells you that the company has robust policies that result in the desired processes, attitudes and behaviours for the company and to promote Ruby would only lead to disturbing the status quo.

67. Bridget enters into a 'full and final' settlement of all claims known at the time of signing the settlement agreement. The respondent has 14 days to pay but decides not to pay Bridget because it says she settled the claims, "so, what's the point?" Advise Bridget.

68. Would your advice to Bridget be different had she entered into a COT3 agreement instead of a settlement agreement?

69. Advise the company on whether it should pay under the settlement agreement.

70. Would your advice be different had they had entered into a COT3 agreement instead of a settlement agreement?

71. As a result of reading this book and the questions, put simply in black and white, has this changed the way you view Race Relations in Employment?

NOTES

NOTES

~ CHAPTER TEN ~

"In a sense, it is a human failure that it should be necessary to proceed by legislation in these matters." Mr Reginald Maudling MP

STATUTES, RULES, REGULATIONS & LINKS

10.1

THE EQUALITY ACT 2010
(KEY EXTRACTS)

PART 2

EQUALITY: KEY CONCEPTS

PROTECTED CHARACTERISTICS

Sections

4. The protected characteristics

The following characteristics are protected characteristics—

...

race

...

9. Race

(1) Race includes—

    (a) colour;

    (b) nationality;

    (c) ethnic or national origins.

(2) In relation to the protected characteristic of race—

(a) a reference to a person who has a particular protected characteristic is a reference to a person of a particular racial group;

(b) a reference to persons who share a protected characteristic is a reference to persons of the same racial group.

(3) A racial group is a group of persons defined by reference to race; and a reference to a person's racial group is a reference to a racial group into which the person falls.

(4) The fact that a racial group comprises two or more distinct racial groups does not prevent it from constituting a particular racial group.

(5) A Minister of the Crown —

(a) must by order amend this section so as to provide for caste to be an aspect of race;

(b) may by order amend this Act so as to provide for an exception to a provision of this Act to apply, or not to apply, to caste or to apply, or not to apply, to caste in specified circumstances.

PROHIBITED CONDUCT

Discrimination

13. Direct discrimination

(1) A person (A) discriminates against another (B) if, because of a protected characteristic, A treats B less favourably than A treats or would treat others.

(5) If the protected characteristic is race, less favourable treatment includes segregating B from others.

19. Indirect discrimination

(1) A person (A) discriminates against another (B) if A applies to B a provision, criterion or practice which is discriminatory in relation to a relevant protected characteristic of B's.

(2) For the purposes of subsection (1), a provision, criterion or practice is discriminatory in relation to a relevant protected characteristic of B's if—

    (a) A applies, or would apply, it to persons with whom B does not share the characteristic,

    (b) it puts, or would put, persons with whom B shares the characteristic at a particular disadvantage when compared with persons with whom B does not share it,

(c) it puts, or would put, B at that disadvantage, and

(d) A cannot show it to be a proportionate means of achieving a legitimate aim.

(3) The relevant protected characteristics are—

…

race

…

23. Comparison by reference to circumstances

(1) On a comparison of cases for the purposes of s.13 […] or 19 there must be no material difference between the circumstances relating to each case.

24. Irrelevance of alleged discriminator's characteristics

(1) For the purpose of establishing a contravention of this Act by virtue of s.13(1), it does not matter whether A has the protected characteristic.

25. References to particular strands of discrimination

(6) Race discrimination is—

(a) discrimination within section 13 because of race;

(b) discrimination within section 19 where the relevant protected characteristic is race.

26. **Harassment**

   (1)   A person (A) harasses another (B) if—

       (a)   A engages in unwanted conduct related to a relevant protected characteristic, and

       (b)   the conduct has the purpose or effect of—

           (i)   violating B's dignity, or

           (ii) creating an intimidating, hostile, degrading, humiliating or offensive environment for B.

   (4)   In deciding whether conduct has the effect referred to in subsection (1)(b), each of the following must be taken into account—

       (a)   the perception of B;

       (b)   the other circumstances of the case;

       (c)   whether it is reasonable for the conduct to have that effect.

   (5)   The relevant protected characteristics are—

   ...

   race

   ...

27. **Victimisation**

   (1)   A person (A) victimises another person (B) if A subjects B to a detriment because—

       (a)   B does a protected act, or

      (b)   A believes that B has done, or may do, a protected act.

(2)   Each of the following is a protected act—
- (a) bringing proceedings under this Act;
- (b) giving evidence or information in connection with proceedings under this Act;
- (c) doing any other thing for the purposes of or in connection with this Act;
- (d) making an allegation (whether or not express) that A or another person has contravened this Act.

(3)   Giving false evidence or information, or making a false allegation, is not a protected act if the evidence or information is given, or the allegation is made, in bad faith.

(4)   This section applies only where the person subjected to a detriment is an individual.

PART 5

EMPLOYMENT, ETC

Employees

39. Employees and applicants

(1) An employer (A) must not discriminate against a person (B)—

    (a) in the arrangements A makes for deciding to whom to offer employment;
    (b) as to the terms on which A offers B employment;
    (c) by not offering B employment.

(2) An employer (A) must not discriminate against an employee of A's (B)—

    (a) as to B's terms of employment;
    (b) in the way A affords B access, or by not affording B access, to opportunities for promotion, transfer or training or for receiving any other benefit, facility or service;
    (c) by dismissing B;
    (d) by subjecting B to any other detriment.

(3) An employer (A) must not victimise a person (B)—

(a) in the arrangements A makes for deciding to whom to offer employment;

(b) as to the terms on which A offers B employment;

(c) by not offering B employment.

(4) An employer (A) must not victimise an employee of A's (B)—

(a) as to B's terms of employment;
(b) in the way A affords B access, or by not affording B access, to opportunities for promotion, transfer or training or for any other benefit, facility or service;

(c) by dismissing B;

(d) by subjecting B to any other detriment.

(7) In subsections (2)(c) and (4)(c), the reference to dismissing B includes a reference to the termination of B's employment—

(a) by the expiry of a period (including a period expiring by reference to an event or circumstance);

(b) by an act of B's (including giving notice) in circumstances such that B is entitled, because of A's conduct, to terminate the employment without notice.

(8) Subsection (7)(a) does not apply if, immediately after the termination, the employment is renewed on the same terms.

40. Employees and applicants: harassment

(1) An employer (A) must not, in relation to employment by A, harass a person (B)—
 (a) who is an employee of A's;
 (b) who has applied to A for employment.

41. Contract workers

(1) A principal must not discriminate against a contract worker—
 (a) as to the terms on which the principal allows the worker to do the work;
 (b) by not allowing the worker to do, or to continue to do, the work;
 (c) in the way the principal affords the worker access, or by not affording the worker access, to opportunities for receiving a benefit, facility or service;
 (d) by subjecting the worker to any other detriment.

(2) A principal must not, in relation to contract work, harass a contract worker.

(3) A principal must not victimise a contract worker—

(a) as to the terms on which the principal allows the worker to do the work;

(b) by not allowing the worker to do, or to continue to do, the work;

(c) in the way the principal affords the worker access, or by not affording the worker access, to opportunities for receiving a benefit, facility or service;

(d) by subjecting the worker to any other detriment.

(4) A duty to make reasonable adjustments applies to a principal (as well as to the employer of a contract worker).

(5) A "principal" is a person who makes work available for an individual who is—

(a) employed by another person, and

(b) supplied by that other person in furtherance of a contract to which the principal is a party (whether or not that other person is a party to it).

(6) "Contract work" is work such as is mentioned in subsection (5).

(7) A "contract worker" is an individual supplied to a principal in furtherance of a contract such as is mentioned in subsection (5)(b).

42. **Identity of employer**

   (1)   For the purposes of this Part, holding the office of constable is to be treated as employment—

      (a)   by the chief officer, in respect of any act done by the chief officer in relation to a constable or appointment to the office of constable;

      (b)   by the responsible authority, in respect of any act done by the authority in relation to a constable or appointment to the office of constable.

44. **Partnerships**

   (1)   A firm or proposed firm must not discriminate against a person—

      (a)   in the arrangements it makes for deciding to whom to offer a position as a partner;

      (b)   as to the terms on which it offers the person a position as a partner;

      (c)   by not offering the person a position as a partner.

   (2)   A firm (A) must not discriminate against a partner (B)—

      (a)   as to the terms on which B is a partner;

(b) in the way A affords B access, or by not affording B access, to opportunities for promotion, transfer or training or for receiving any other benefit, facility or service;

(c) by expelling B;

(d) by subjecting B to any other detriment.

(3) A firm must not, in relation to a position as a partner, harass—

(a) a partner;

(b) a person who has applied for the position.

(4) A proposed firm must not, in relation to a position as a partner, harass a person who has applied for the position.

(5) A firm or proposed firm must not victimise a person—

(a) in the arrangements it makes for deciding to whom to offer a position as a partner;

(b) as to the terms on which it offers the person a position as a partner;

(c) by not offering the person a position as a partner.

(6) A firm (A) must not victimise a partner (B)—

(a) as to the terms on which B is a partner;

(b) in the way A affords B access, or by not affording B access, to opportunities for promotion, transfer or training or for receiving any other benefit, facility or service;

(c) by expelling B;

(d) by subjecting B to any other detriment.

(8) In the application of this section to a limited partnership within the meaning of the Limited Partnerships Act 1907, "partner" means a general partner within the meaning of that Act.

45. Limited liability partnerships

(1) An LLP or proposed LLP must not discriminate against a person—

(a) in the arrangements it makes for deciding to whom to offer a position as a member;
(b) as to the terms on which it offers the person a position as a member;

(c) by not offering the person a position as a member.

(2) An LLP (A) must not discriminate against a member (B)—

(a) as to the terms on which B is a member;
(b) in the way A affords B access, or by not affording B access, to opportunities for promotion, transfer or training or for

receiving any other benefit, facility or service;

(c) by expelling B;

(d) by subjecting B to any other detriment.

(3) An LLP must not, in relation to a position as a member, harass—

(a) a member;

(b) a person who has applied for the position.

(4) A proposed LLP must not, in relation to a position as a member, harass a person who has applied for the position.

(5) An LLP or proposed LLP must not victimise a person—

(a) in the arrangements it makes for deciding to whom to offer a position as a member;

(b) as to the terms on which it offers the person a position as a member;

(c) by not offering the person a position as a member.

(6) An LLP (A) must not victimise a member (B)—

(a) as to the terms on which B is a member;

(b) in the way A affords B access, or by not affording B access, to opportunities for promotion, transfer or training or for receiving any other benefit, facility or service;

(c)　by expelling B;

(d)　by subjecting B to any other detriment.

50.　Public offices: appointments etc.

[Not reproduced]

51.　Public offices: recommendations for appointments, etc.

[Not reproduced]

53.　Qualifying bodies

(1)　A qualifications body (A) must not discriminate against a person (B)—

(a)　in the arrangements A makes for deciding upon whom to confer a relevant qualification;

(b)　as to the terms on which it is prepared to confer a relevant qualification on B;

(c)　by not conferring a relevant qualification on B.

(2)　A qualifications body (A) must not discriminate against a person (B) upon whom A has conferred a relevant qualification—

(a)　by withdrawing the qualification from B;

(b) by varying the terms on which B holds the qualification;

(c) by subjecting B to any other detriment.

(3) A qualifications body must not, in relation to conferment by it of a relevant qualification, harass—

(a) a person who holds the qualification, or

(b) a person who applies for it.

(4) A qualifications body (A) must not victimise a person (B)—

(a) in the arrangements A makes for deciding upon whom to confer a relevant qualification;

(b) as to the terms on which it is prepared to confer a relevant qualification on B;

(c) by not conferring a relevant qualification on B.

(5) A qualifications body (A) must not victimise a person (B) upon whom A has conferred a relevant qualification—

(a) by withdrawing the qualification from B;

(b) by varying the terms on which B holds the qualification;

(c) by subjecting B to any other detriment.

55. Employment service-providers

(1) A person (an "employment service-provider") concerned with the provision of an employment service must not discriminate against a person—

   (a) in the arrangements the service-provider makes for selecting persons to whom to provide, or to whom to offer to provide, the service;

   (b) as to the terms on which the service-provider offers to provide the service to the person;

   (c) by not offering to provide the service to the person.

(2) An employment service-provider (A) must not, in relation to the provision of an employment service, discriminate against a person (B)—

   (a) as to the terms on which A provides the service to B;
   (b) by not providing the service to B;
   (c) by terminating the provision of the service to B;
   (d) by subjecting B to any other detriment.

(3) An employment service-provider must not, in relation to the provision of an employment service, harass—

(a) a person who asks the service-provider to provide the service;

(b) a person for whom the service-provider provides the service.

(4) An employment service-provider (A) must not victimise a person (B)—

    (a) in the arrangements A makes for selecting persons to whom to provide, or to whom to offer to provide, the service;

    (b) as to the terms on which A offers to provide the service to

    B;

    (c) by not offering to provide the service to B.

(5) An employment service-provider (A) must not, in relation to the provision of an employment service, victimise a person (B)—

    (a) as to the terms on which A provides the service to B;

    (b) by not providing the service to B;

    (c) by terminating the provision of the service to B;

    (d) by subjecting B to any other detriment.

83. Interpretation and exceptions

(1) This section applies for the purposes of this Part.

(2) "Employment" means—

(a) employment under a contract of employment, a contract of apprenticeship or a contract personally to do work;

PART 8

PROHIBITED CONDUCT: ANCILLARY

108. Relationships that have ended

(1) A person (A) must not discriminate against another (B) if—

(a) the discrimination arises out of and is closely connected to a relationship which used to exist between them, and

(b) conduct of a description constituting the discrimination would, if it occurred during the relationship, contravene this Act.

(2) A person (A) must not harass another (B) if—

(a) the harassment arises out of and is closely connected to a relationship which used to exist between them, and

(b) conduct of a description constituting the harassment would, if it occurred during the relationship, contravene this Act.

(3) It does not matter whether the relationship ends before or after the commencement of this section.

(6) For the purposes of Part 9 (enforcement), a contravention of this section relates to the Part of this Act that would have been contravened if the relationship had not ended.

(7) But conduct is not a contravention of this section in so far as it also amounts to victimisation of B by A.

109. Liability of employers and principals

(1) Anything done by a person (A) in the course of A's employment must be treated as also done by the employer.

(2) Anything done by an agent for a principal, with the authority of the principal, must be treated as also done by the principal.

(3) It does not matter whether that thing is done with the employer's or principal's knowledge or approval.

(4) In proceedings against A's employer (B) in respect of anything alleged to have been done by A in the course of A's employment it is a defence for B to

show that B took all reasonable steps to prevent A—

(a) from doing that thing, or
(b) from doing anything of that description.

(5) This section does not apply to offences under this Act […]

PART 9

ENFORCEMENT

INTRODUCTORY

110. **Liability of employees and agents**

(1) A person (A) contravenes this section if—
   (a) A is an employee or agent,
   (b) A does something which, by virtue of s.109(1) or (2), is treated as having been done by A's employer or principal (as the case may be), and
   (c) the doing of that thing by A amounts to a contravention of this Act by the employer or principal (as the case may be).

(2) It does not matter whether, in any proceedings, the employer is found not to have contravened this Act by virtue of s.109(4).

(3) A does not contravene this section if—

   (a) A relies on a statement by the employer or principal that doing that thing is not a contravention of this Act, and

   (b) it is reasonable for A to do so.

(4) A person (B) commits an offence if B knowingly or recklessly makes a statement mentioned in subsection (3)(a) which is false or misleading in a material respect.

(5) A person guilty of an offence under subsection (4) is liable on summary conviction to a fine not exceeding level 5 on the standard scale.

112. Aiding contraventions

(1) A person (A) must not knowingly help another (B) to do anything which contravenes Part 3, 4, 5, 6 or 7 or section 108(1) or (2) or 111 (a basic contravention).

(2) It is not a contravention of subsection (1) if—

   (a) A relies on a statement by B that the act for which the help is given does not contravene this Act, and

   (b) it is reasonable for A to do so.

(3) B commits an offence if B knowingly or recklessly makes a statement mentioned in subsection (2)(a) which is false or misleading in a material respect.

(4) A person guilty of an offence under subsection (3) is liable on summary conviction to a fine not exceeding level 5 on the standard scale.

(5) For the purposes of Part 9 (enforcement), a contravention of this section is to be treated as relating to the provision of this Act to which the basic contravention relates.

(6) The reference in subsection (1) to a basic contravention does not include a reference to disability discrimination in contravention of Chapter 1 of Part 6 (schools).

119. Remedies

(4) An award of damages may include compensation for injured feelings (whether or not it includes compensation on any other basis).

EMPLOYMENT TRIBUNALS

120. Jurisdiction

(1) An employment tribunal has, subject to s.121 [Armed Forces Case], jurisdiction to determine a complaint relating to—
 (a) a contravention of Part 5 (work);
 (b) a contravention of section 108 [...]

(7) s.120(1)(a) does not apply to a contravention of s.53 in so far as the act complained of may, by

virtue of an enactment, be subject to an appeal or proceedings in the nature of an appeal.

123. Time limits

(1) […] proceedings on a complaint within s.120 may not be brought after the end of—

    (a) the period of 3 months starting with the date of the act to which the complaint relates, or

    (b) such other period as the employment tribunal thinks just and equitable.

(3) For the purposes of this section—

    (a) conduct extending over a period is to be treated as done at the end of the period;

    (b) failure to do something is to be treated as occurring when the person in question decided on it.

(4) In the absence of evidence to the contrary, a person (P) is to be taken to decide on failure to do something—

    (a) when P does an act inconsistent with doing it, or

    (b) if P does no inconsistent act, on the expiry of the period in which P might reasonably have been expected to do it.

124. Remedies: general

(1) This section applies if an employment tribunal finds that there has been a contravention of a provision referred to in s.120(1).

(2) The tribunal may—

    (a) make a declaration as to the rights of the complainant and the respondent in relation to the matters to which the proceedings relate;

    (b) order the respondent to pay compensation to the complainant;

    (c) make an appropriate recommendation.

(3) An appropriate recommendation is a recommendation that within a specified period the respondent takes specified steps for the purpose of obviating or reducing the adverse effect on the complainant of any matter to which the proceedings relate—

(4) Subsection (5) applies if the tribunal—

    (a) finds that a contravention is established by virtue of s.19, but

    (b) is satisfied that the provision, criterion or practice was not applied with the intention of discriminating against the complainant.

(5) It must not make an order under subsection (2)(b) unless it first considers whether to act under subsection (2)(a) or (c).

(6) The amount of compensation which may be awarded under subsection (2)(b) corresponds to the amount which could be awarded by the county court […]

(7) If a respondent fails, without reasonable excuse, to comply with an appropriate recommendation…the tribunal may—

    (a) if an order was made under subsection (2)(b), increase the amount of compensation to be paid;

    (b) if no such order was made, make one.

MISCELLANEOUS

136. Burden of proof

(1) This section applies to any proceedings relating to a contravention of this Act.

(2) If there are facts from which the court could decide, in the absence of any other explanation, that a person (A) contravened the provision concerned, the court must hold that the contravention occurred.

(3) But subsection (2) does not apply if A shows that A did not contravene the provision.

(5) This section does not apply to proceedings for an offence under this Act.

(6) A reference to the court includes a reference to—

(a) an employment tribunal;

147. Meaning of "qualifying settlement agreement"

(1) This section applies for the purposes of this Part.

(2) A qualifying settlement agreement is a contract in relation to which each of the conditions in subsection (3) is met.

(3) Those conditions are that—

(a) the contract is in writing,

(b) the contract relates to the particular complaint,

(c) the complainant has, before entering into the contract, received advice from an independent adviser about its terms and effect (including, in particular, its effect on the complainant's ability to pursue the complaint before an employment tribunal),

(d) on the date of the giving of the advice, there is in force a contract of insurance, or an indemnity provided for members of a profession or professional body, covering the risk of a claim by the complainant in respect of loss arising from the advice,

(e) the contract identifies the adviser, and

(f) the contract states that the conditions in paragraphs (c) and (d) are met.

(4) Each of the following is an independent adviser—

(a) a qualified lawyer;

(b) an officer, official, employee or member of an independent trade union certified in writing by the trade union as competent to give advice and as authorised to do so on its behalf;

(c) a worker at an advice centre (whether as an employee or a volunteer) certified in writing by the centre as competent to give advice and as authorised to do so on its behalf;

(d) a person of such description as may be specified by order.

(5) Despite subsection (4), none of the following is an independent adviser to the complainant in relation to a qualifying settlement agreement—

    (a) a person (other than the complainant) who is a party to the contract or the complaint;

    (b) a person who is connected to a person within paragraph (a);

    (c) a person who is employed by a person within paragraph (a) or (b);

    (d) a person who is acting for a person within paragraph (a) or (b) in relation to the contract or the complaint;

    (e) a person within subsection (4)(b) or (c), if the trade union or advice centre is a person within paragraph (a) or (b);

    (f) a person within subsection (4)(c) to whom the complainant makes a payment for the advice.

(6) A "qualified lawyer", for the purposes of subsection (4)(a), is—

    (a) in relation to England and Wales, a person who, for the purposes of the Legal Services Act 2007, is an authorised person in relation to an activity which constitutes the exercise of a right of audience or the conduct of litigation;

    (b) in relation to Scotland, an advocate (whether in practice as such or employed to give legal advice) or a solicitor who holds a practising certificate.

(7) "Independent trade union" has the meaning given in section 5 of the Trade Union and Labour Relations (Consolidation) Act 1992.

(8) Two persons are connected for the purposes of subsection (5) if—

(a) one is a company of which the other (directly or indirectly) has control, or

(b) both are companies of which a third person (directly or indirectly) has control.

(9) Two persons are also connected for the purposes of subsection (5) in so far as a connection between them gives rise to a conflict of interest in relation to the contract or the complaint.

10.2

EMPLOYMENT TRIBUNALS ACT 1996 – ACAS CERTIFICATE

BEFORE INSTITUTING PROCEEDINGS

18A. Requirement to contact ACAS before instituting proceedings

(1) Before a person ("the prospective claimant") presents an application to institute relevant proceedings relating to any matter, the prospective claimant must provide to ACAS prescribed

information, in the prescribed manner, about that matter…

21. **Jurisdiction of Appeal Tribunal**
    (1) An appeal lies to the Appeal Tribunal on any question of law arising from any decision of, or arising in any proceedings before an employment tribunal under or by virtue of–
    (ge) the Equality Act 2010.

10.3
EMPLOYMENT APPEAL TRIBUNAL RULES 1993

2. **Institution of Appeal**
    (3) The period within which an appeal to the Appeal Tribunal may be instituted is–(a) in the case of an appeal from a judgment of the employment tribunal–
    (i) where the written reasons for the judgment subject to appeal–
    (aa) were requested orally at the hearing before the employment tribunal or in writing within 14 days of the date on which the written record of the judgment was sent to the parties; or
    (bb) were reserved and given in writing by the employment tribunal 42 days from the date on which the written reasons were sent to the parties;
    (ii) …; or

(iii) where the written reasons for the judgment subject to appeal–

(aa) were not requested orally at the hearing before the employment tribunal or in writing within 14 days of the date on which the written record of the judgment was sent to the parties; and

(bb) were not reserved and given in writing by the employment tribunal

42 days from the date on which the written record of the

judgment was sent to the parties;

10.4

THE EMPLOYMENT TRIBUNALS RULES OF PROCEDURE 2013, SCHEDULE 1

2. Overriding objective

The overriding objective of these Rules is to enable Employment Tribunals to deal with cases fairly and justly. Dealing with a case fairly and justly includes, so far as practicable—

(a) ensuring that the parties are on an equal footing;

(b) dealing with cases in ways which are proportionate to the complexity and importance of the issues;

(c) avoiding unnecessary formality and seeking flexibility in the proceedings;

(d) avoiding delay, so far as compatible with proper consideration of the issues; and

(e) saving expense.

A Tribunal shall seek to give effect to the overriding objective in interpreting, or exercising any power given to it by, these Rules. The parties and their representatives shall assist the Tribunal to further the overriding objective and in particular shall co-operate generally with each other and with the Tribunal.

3. **Alternative dispute resolution**
A Tribunal shall wherever practicable and appropriate encourage the use by the parties of the services of ACAS, judicial or other mediation, or other means of resolving their disputes by agreement.

8. **Presenting the claim**
(1) A claim shall be started by presenting a completed claim form (using a prescribed form)…

37. **Striking out**
(1) At any stage of the proceedings, either on its own initiative or on the application of a party, a Tribunal

may strike out all or part of a claim or response on any of the following grounds—

(a) that it is scandalous or vexatious or has no reasonable prospect of success;

(b) that the manner in which the proceedings have been conducted by or on behalf of the claimant or the respondent (as the case may be) has been scandalous, unreasonable or vexatious;

(c) for non-compliance with any of these Rules or with an order of the Tribunal;

(d) that it has not been actively pursued;

(e) that the Tribunal considers that it is no longer possible to have a fair hearing in respect of the claim or response (or the part to be struck out).

(2) A claim or response may not be struck out unless the party in question has been given a reasonable opportunity to make representations, either in writing or, if requested by the party, at a hearing.

(3) Where a response is struck out, the effect shall be as if no response had been presented, as set out in rule 21 above.[249]

39. Deposit orders

---

[249] "Effect of non-representation or rejection of response, or case not contested"

(1) Where at a preliminary hearing (under rule 53) the Tribunal considers that any specific allegation or argument in a claim or response has little reasonable prospect of success, it may make an order requiring a party ("the paying party") to pay a deposit not exceeding £1,000 as a condition of continuing to advance that allegation or argument.

(2) The Tribunal shall make reasonable enquiries into the paying party's ability to pay the deposit and have regard to any such information when deciding the amount of the deposit.

(3) The Tribunal's reasons for making the deposit order shall be provided with the order and the paying party must be notified about the potential consequences of the order.

(4) If the paying party fails to pay the deposit by the date specified the specific allegation or argument to which the deposit order relates shall be struck out. Where a response is struck out, the consequences shall be as if no response had been presented, as set out in rule 21.

(5)…

(6)…

61. Decisions made at or following a hearing

(1) Where there is a hearing the Tribunal may either announce its decision in relation to any issue at the

hearing or reserve it to be sent to the parties as soon as practicable in writing.

(2) If the decision is announced at the hearing, a written record (in the form of a judgment if appropriate) shall be provided to the parties (and, where the proceedings were referred to the Tribunal by a court, to that court) as soon as practicable. (Decisions concerned only with the conduct of a hearing need not be identified in the record of that hearing unless a party requests that a specific decision is so recorded.)

(3) The written record shall be signed by the Employment Judge.

62. Reasons

(1) The Tribunal shall give reasons for its decision on any disputed issue, whether substantive or procedural (including any decision on an application for reconsideration or for orders for costs, preparation time or wasted costs).

(2) In the case of a decision given in writing the reasons shall also be given in writing. In the case of a decision announced at a hearing the reasons may be given orally at the hearing or reserved to be given in writing later (which may, but need not, be as part of the written record of the decision). Written reasons shall be signed by the Employment Judge.

(3) Where reasons have been given orally, the Employment Judge shall announce that written reasons will not be provided unless they are asked for by any party at the hearing itself or by a written request presented by any party within 14 days of the sending of the written record of the decision. The written record of the decision shall repeat that information. If no such request is received, the Tribunal shall provide written reasons only if requested to do so by the Employment Appeal Tribunal or a court.

(4) The reasons given for any decision shall be proportionate to the significance of the issue and for decisions other than judgments may be very short.

(5) In the case of a judgment the reasons shall: identify the issues which the Tribunal has determined, state the findings of fact made in relation to those issues, concisely identify the relevant law, and state how that law has been applied to those findings in order to decide the issues. Where the judgment includes a financial award the reasons shall identify, by means of a table or otherwise, how the amount to be paid has been calculated.

RECONSIDERATION OF JUDGMENTS

70. **Principles**

A Tribunal may, either on its own initiative (which may reflect a request from the Employment Appeal Tribunal) or on the application of a party, reconsider any judgment where it is necessary in the interests of justice to do so. On reconsideration, the decision ("the original decision") may be confirmed, varied or revoked. If it is revoked it may be taken again.

71. Application

Except where it is made in the course of a hearing, an application for reconsideration shall be presented in writing (and copied to all the other parties) within 14 days of the date on which the written record, or other written communication, of the original decision was sent to the parties or within 14 days of the date that the written reasons were sent (if later) and shall set out why reconsideration of the original decision is necessary.

10.5
WEBSITES

ACAS
https://www.acas.org.uk

British and Irish Legal Information Institute
https://www.bailii.org

Citizens Advice
https://www.citizensadvice.org.uk

Employment Appeal Tribunal Forms
https://www.gov.uk/government/collections/employment-appeal-tribunal-forms

Employment Tribunal Forms and Guidance
https://www.gov.uk/government/collections/employment-tribunal-forms

Employment Tribunal Procedure Rules
https://www.gov.uk/government/publications/employment-tribunal-procedure-rules

Equality and Human Rights Commission
https://www.equalityhumanrights.com/en

Information Commissioner's Office
https://ico.org.uk

United Kingdom Legislations
https://www.legislation.gov.uk

Ryan Clement

https://www.ryanclement.com

https://www.youtube.com/@RyanClement1/

INDEX

ACAS Code of Practice on Disciplinary & Grievance Procedure, **3.4-6**

ACAS (COT3), **6.22**

ACAS (certificate), **4.3, 4.7**

ACAS (notifying), **4.31**

ACAS Guide, Disciplinary & Grievance at Work, **3.4**

Aggravated damages, **6.40**

Afzal, Nazir, **8.12**

Ahmed, Jahid, **8.18**

Appeal from Employment Tribunal to Employment Appeal Tribunal, **6.46-47**

Badenoch, Kemi, **1.18**

Baird, John, **1.2**

Barnes, John, **8.7**

Because of a protected characteristic, **2.15-17**

Bell, Ronald, **1.1**

Benn, Anthony, **1.1**

Black Lives Matter, **1.19**

Braine, Bernard, **1.2**

Brennan, Kevin, **8.16**

British Broadcasting Corporation, **7.9**

Brixton riots (Scarman report into), **8.24**

Lord Brockway, Fenner, **1.1-5, 1.7, 8.1**

Burden of proof, **6.14**

Butler, R.A., **1.4**

Callaghan, James, **1.8-10, 1.16**

Calvert-Smith, Sir David, **8.14-15**

Carmichael, Stokey and Hamilton, Charles V., **8.2**

Baroness Casey of Blackstock, Louise, **8.1**

Cashmore, Ellis, **8.23**

Caste, **2.12**

Castle, Barbara, **1.1**

Cochrane, Kelso, **1.4, 1.13**

Colour, **2.11**

Commission on Race and Ethnic Disparities: The Report, **1.18**

Conduct done in the course of employment, **3.34**

Conscious, **9.4-5, 9.7**

Context (harassment), **2.38-2.42**

Contractual and Non-Contractual Procedure (Grievance), **3.9-10**

COT3, **6.22**

Crown Prosecution Service (CPS), **8.14-15**

Deposit orders, **6.9**

Digital, Culture, Media and Sport Committee, **8.14-18,**

Direct Discrimination, **2.13-21, 4.18-19**

Direct Discrimination and Victimisation, **2.49-50**

Disciplinary Procedure and Process, **3.27-33**

Disclosure, **p171**

Diversity Awareness & Inclusion, **7.1-14**

DNA, **7.5**

Dobell, George, **8.18**

Elliott, Julie, **8.18**

Employer's liability, **4.34**

Employment Appeal Tribunal Rules 1993, **10.3**

Employment Tribunal, **4.1-37, 6.1-6.47**

Employment Tribunal (Balance the injustice and hardship), **5.22**

Employment Tribunal (bundle), **6.13**

Employment Tribunal (burden of proof), **6.14**

Employment Tribunal (Claim Form - ET1), **4.9-11**

Employment Tribunal (deposit order), **6.9**

Employment Tribunal (disclosure), **6.11-12**

Employment Tribunal (Entirely New Claim), **5.14, 5.21-23**

Employment Tribunal (hearing), **6.27-37**

Employment Tribunal (Judicial Mediation), **6.17, 6.19-20**

Employment Tribunal (Jurisdiction – discrimination by non-employers), **4.38-41**

Employment Tribunal (list of issues), **6.4-8**

Employment Tribunal (Orders), **6.10**

Employment Tribunal (Overriding objective), **6.2**

Employment Tribunal (Reconsideration), **6.45**

Employment Tribunal (Relabelling Exercise), **5.15-20**

Employment Tribunal (remedy), **6.38-44**

Employment Tribunal (Response - ET3), **4.12-14**

Employment Tribunal (strike out), **6.9**

Employment Tribunal (Territorial Jurisdiction), **4.37**

Employment Tribunal (three months less 1 day), **4.5-8, 5.23**

Employment Tribunal (time limits), **4.4**

Employment Tribunal (witness statements), **6.14-16**

Employment Tribunals Act 1996 – ACAS Certificate before instituting proceedings, **10.2**

Employment Tribunals Rules of Procedure 2013, Schedule 1, **10.4**

England and Wales Cricket Board (ECB), **8.22, 8.35, 8.36**

England National Football Team, **1.19**

Equality Act 2010, **2.1-51**

Equality Act 2010 (Key Extracts), **10.1**

Error of Law, **6.46-47**

Essex County Cricket Club, **8.18, 8.36**

Ethnicity, **2.6-9**

Fisher, **1.4**

Foot, Sir Dingle, **1.6-7, 1.9**

Football fans, **1.19**

Green, Damian, **8.15**

Grievance, **3.1-13, 3.16-19**

Grievance & Disciplinary, **3.1**

Grievance Letter, **3.23-24**

Grievance Process and Procedure, **3.20-22**

Grounds of Complaint, **5.2-3, 5.5-6, 5.8-9, 5.11-12**

Grounds of Resistance, **5.2, 5.4-5, 5.7-8, 5.10-11, 5.13**

Harassment, **2.32-42, 4.24-28**

Harassment and Direct Discrimination, **2.43**

Hearing (Employment Tribunal), **6.27-37**

Herbert, Peter, **8.34**

Hutton, Roger, **8.13, 8.16-17, 8.19**

Institute of Race Relations, **9.13**

Impartiality, **3.8**

Inclusion, **7.8-7.14**

Indirect Discrimination, **2.22-27, 4.20-23**

Indirect Discrimination compared with Discrimination, **2.28-31**

Institutional Racism, **2.52-53, 8.1-38**

Investigation (disciplinary), **3.30**

Invitation to Disciplinary Letter, **3.26**

Jenkins, Roy, **1.11**
Johnson, Boris, **1.18**
Dr Jones, Steve, **2.3**
Judicial Mediation, **6.19-20**
Justification, **2.30-31**

Knight, Julian, **8.13**

Lawrence, Stephen, **1.13**
Less favourable treatment, **2.18-21**
List of issues (Claims 1-4), **6.4-8**
London Fire Brigade (Independent Culture Review), **8.12**
Lopez MP, Julia, **9.14**

Macpherson, Sir William, **1.13**
Macpherson Inquiry, **1.13**
Macpherson Report, **1.14, 2.52, 8.3-4, 8.28**
The McGregor-Smith Review, **1.17**
Mediation, **6.17-20**
Mediation in the workplace, **6.18**
Metropolitan Police, **8.1**

Nationality and National Origin, **2.10**

NHS England and NHS Improvement Commissioning, **8.1**

Lord Patel of Bradford, Kamlesh, **8.13, 8.16-17, 8.21**

PCP (Provision, Criterion or Practice), **2.24-27**

Pleadings, **4.15-17, 5.1-13**

Positive action, **7.9-13**

Positive discrimination, **7.9**

Prescod, Colin, **9.13**

Lord Prior, David, **1.17**

Protected act, **2.45-48**

Provision, Criterion and Practice, **2.24-27**

Purpose or effect of the conduct (harassment), **2.35-37**

Questions, **9.16**

Race, **2.2-12**

Racial Group, **2.4-5**

Racism and Race Discrimination, **2.51**

Racist abuse, **1.19**

Rafiq, Azim, **8.2, 8.13-15**

Reconsideration and Appeal (EAT), **6.45-47**

Remedy, **6.38-44**

Right to have grievance heard, **3.7**

Rowley, Sir Mark, **8.27**

Lord Scarman, **8.3, 8.34**
Scarman Report, **8.3, 8.24**
Schedule of loss, **6.43**
Scottish cricket (Independent review into racism), **8.8-11**
Settlement Agreement, **6.22.4, 6.25**
Sewell Report, **1.18, 8.25**
Dr Sewell, Tony, **1.18**
Silverman, S, **1.4**
Social Construct, **7.5-7.7**
Soskice, Sir Frank, **1.6**
Sportscotland, **8.8-11**
Statement of Particulars of Employment, **3.14-3.15**
Statutes, Rules, Regulations & Links, **10.1-4**
Statutory Defence, **4.35-36**
Stoneham, Lord, **1.6**
Straw, Jack, **1.15**
Strike out, **6.9**
Structural racism, **8.25**
Subconscious, **9.2, 9.4-7**
Systemic racism, **8.25**

Taking the Knee, **1.19**

Territorial Jurisdiction, **4.37**

Training, **9.13**

Unconscious, **9.2, 9.4, 9.6, 9.8-9**

Unconscious bias, **9.8-12**

Unwanted conduct by whom (harassment)? **2.33-34**

Victimisation, **2.44-2.48, 4.29-33**

Websites, **10.5**

Without prejudice offers, **6.21-25**

Without prejudice save as to costs, **6.26**

Witness statements, **6.14-16**

Lord Woolley, Simon, **1.18-19**

Written Grievance Procedure, **3.11**

(No) Written Grievance Procedure, **3.12-13**

Yorkshire County Cricket Club, **8.2, 8.13-22**

Young, Hugo, **8.6**

Printed in Great Britain
by Amazon